Beyond Rights Talk and Culture Talk

Good Summaries
in Introduction

Beyond Rights Talk and Culture Talk

Comparative Essays
on the Politics of Rights and Culture

Mahmood Mamdani

ST. MARTIN'S PRESS
New York
2000

St. Martin's Press, Scholarly and Reference Division,
175 Fifth Avenue, New York, N.Y. 10010

First published in the United States of America in 2000

Printed in South Africa by The Rustica Press, Old Mill Road, Ndabeni, Cape Town
D8065

ISBN: 0-312-23497-X (cloth)
ISBN: 0-312-23498-8 (paper)

Cover design by Sarah-Anne Raynham
Cover art by kind permission of the South African Museum (SAM AE 4869, Luvale cultural group, 'Barotseland', Zambia, 1926); photo by Herschel Mair

Library of Congress Cataloging-in-Publication Data

Beyond rights talk and culture talk : comparative essays on the politics of rights and culture / edited by Mahmood Mamdani.
        p. cm.
    Includes bibliographical references and index.
    ISBN 0-312-23497-X (cloth) -- ISBN 0-312-23498-8 (paper)
        1. Human rights. 2. Culture. I. Mamdani, Mahmood, 1946-

JC571.B49 2000
323--dc21
                                                                00-027821

Contents

Contributors

Hussaina J Abdullah, a Nigerian sociologist, is an independent consultant and researcher living in Uppsala, Sweden.

Martin Chanock is Professor of Law and Legal Studies at La Trobe University in Melbourne.

Kimberle Crenshaw is Professor of Law at Columbia University.

Mahmood Mamdani is Herbert Lehman Professor of Government at Columbia University.

Nivedita Menon is Lecturer in Political Science in Lady Shri Ram College in New Delhi.

Ebrahim Moosa is a faculty memeber of the Department of Religious Studies at the University of Cape Town.

Thandabantu Nhlapo is Professor of Private Law at the University of Cape Town.

Issa G Shivji is Professor of Law at the University of Dar es Salaam.

Introduction

Mahmood Mamdani

Imagine that a man slaps a woman in rural KwaZulu-Natal, South Africa. At the same time, another man slaps a woman in a popular neighbourhood in Khartoum, and yet a third does the same in a classroom at the Sorbonne in Paris. All three women protest: the woman in Paris that her rights have been violated, the woman in Khartoum that her dignity has been violated, and the woman in KwaZulu-Natal that custom has been violated. Every victim protests. But the language of protest is different in each case. How is one to understand this difference?

The language of protest, I will argue, bears a relationship to the language of power. To understand why protest employs the language of rights in Paris, dignity in Khartoum, and custom in KwaZulu-Natal, it is worth recalling that power claims to uphold rights in Paris, dignity in Khartoum and custom in KwaZulu-Natal. Is not the starting point of protest to take power at face value, and to question its claim and thus legitimacy?

How significant is the difference in language? The debate at the conference on Cultural Transformations – held at the Centre for African Studies at the University of Cape Town[1] – unfolded with a discussion of the languages of rights and culture (rights talk and culture talk). This volume contains a selection of the papers presented at the conference. In choosing the papers, I have tried to identify those which best present the different sides of the conference discussion. Rather than choosing and defending one side of the debate, I shall try to map the issues that drove the debate and are worked out in greater detail in the essays that follow.

Rights talk and culture talk: Martin Chanock and Thandabantu Nhlapo

In retrospect, two papers set the terms of the conference debate: one was by Martin Chanock, the other by Thandabantu Nhlapo. They form the opening and closing chapters of this volume. Both try to think through the relationship between the language of culture and that of rights. In the process, they come to strikingly different conclusions.

Martin Chanock turns to the history of cultural change in the West to underline the universal aspect of economic change and to draw out its non-economic consequences. He encapsulates this history in two different transitions, one socio-economic, the other political. The socio-economic transition is that from agrarian to industrial society. Chanock thinks this 'great transformation' – to use Karl Polanyi's well-known characterisation of it – led to nothing less than a shift in cultural consensus in the West. That current occidentalising thought from the non-West tends to transmute this outcome into an ahistorical cultural divide between the West and the rest clearly unmasks its demagogic character.

Chanock describes the political transition as having occurred in two phases. The first was born in the throes of religious conflict in Europe. Ironically, it is the struggle for religious equality that led to the creation of a secular political community through the taming of religion. Instead of being religiously based as before, the secular political community was based on either kin or contractual relations. Its basis was either ethnic or civic. The second phase of cultural transformation was the consequence of a different struggle, one for colour and gender equality. Each of these transformations was born of political conflict, not of a cultural consensus. Not surprisingly, each is described in the language of rights, not culture. It is the universalising potential of rights – as opposed to any claim for its universal validity – that Chanock asks his audience to consider seriously. And it is the parochial dimension of culture talk that he questions as masking a defence of local privilege.

Culture talk, Chanock argues, had some legitimacy in the colonial context, but no longer. Today, culture has become a language of rulers, particularly in the ex-colonial world. Part of the intellectual history of empire, the history of its decolonisation, is a shift from using race to using culture to describe difference. Thus Chanock's 'framing question': How and when did culture become the primary way of describing difference? For Chanock, the answer lies in a coincidence of two processes, political decolonisation and economic change. Of the two, material process is key to explaining the shift.

The language of cultural authenticity, Chanock argues, is born of a dual context, external and internal. At a time when the authority of national elites is being eroded by market-based changes, it privileges an elite understanding of culture internally. The market has rendered volatile the relations between genders and generations. Correspondingly, it is those branches of law – such as family and land law – that fall within the realm of culture wherein these tensions are most expressed.

Externally, the process of globalisation has put national elites under increas-ing pressure. One after another, each group has been subjected to a Structural-Adjustment Programme and has been deprived of state resources that have func-tioned as a pork barrel for patronage. Their response has been demagogic: on the one hand, to accent social–economic as opposed to civil–political rights, and group as opposed to individual rights; on the other, to lean on cultural difference to question the universalising potential of rights. The simple fact, Chanock argues, is that while the international market universalises consumption, nation-al elites emphasise continued difference: occidentalising is simply the other side of orientalising. Chanock closes with a plea for universalisation, as aspiration as opposed to reality. Specifically, he calls for a universalisation of rights culture at the national level, to counter both the demagogy of local ruling classes, and the threat of fragmentation posed by community-based elites.

The essay raises an important question as it moves from an analytical to a pre-scriptive mode. If local culture – whether national or community-based – is nothing but a demagogic posture of dominant local interests under assault by market forces, why does it resonate with others beyond their narrow confines? It is this question that Thandabantu Nhlapo raises in the concluding essay. Western culture, Nhlapo observes, is powerful, transportable, flexible, all-pervasive. Born of the womb of Western culture, the rights movement is intolerant of competing world-views. Its clout and its cocksureness make it as great a threat to democra-tic values as any despot in a multi-cultural context.

Part of the self-righteousness and intolerance of the rights movement is its tendency to dismiss every local cultural assertion as masking a defence of privi-lege and inequality at the expense of the individual rights of the disadvantaged in the same society. Nhlapo has two responses to the rights critique. He does not deny that the language of culture may indeed mask a defence of privilege at cer-tain times. But he is wary of the kind of one-eyed glimpse that sees privilege only in someone else's front yard, and thus concludes that every attempt to use a dif-ferent yardstick is nothing but a defence of privilege.

Rather than denying the existence of local privilege, Nhlapo calls attention to 'concentric circles of privilege'. The inference is that those who habitually point to local privilege risk becoming blind to global privilege and turning into its local apologists. For Nhlapo culture talk involves more than just a defence of local privilege: the very upholding of one's dignity – a right according to the South African Constitution – requires a defence of one's culture, particularly of the points of difference in it. It is from this point of view, he argues, that a rights critique of this same local culture represents no more than a culture-bound Western assault on local dignity. To underline the point, he provides illustrations. What should be our attitude to, say, a religion according to the tenets of which women cannot conduct ceremonies that male church leaders conduct? How different is that from the practice of polygyny and *lobolo* in Africa?

Nhlapo's general point is this: the question of dignity is constitutionally guaranteed, and yet it is entirely subjective. The dignity of local cultures requires their constitutional protection – except when particular practices can be shown to cause harm to particular members of the community. The protection of dignity requires that diversity be ensured, and this is why general demands for the provision of equality must be balanced with the specific recognition of difference.

The encounter between these two essays raises a series of questions of relevance to the subject matter of this volume. If culture talk involves more than just a defence of local privilege, then does not rights talk also involve more than just a Western cultural assertion? To the extent that culture talk is about dignity and difference, and rights talk about equality and sameness, do we not need a language other than that of the law to express difference? Finally, how do we ensure that those who claim to safeguard cultural difference do not turn around to impose a cultural dictatorship on their own communities? Put differently, how do we ensure diversity – not just *between* cultures but also *within* cultures – and thus free play for those forces that give cultures their internal dynamism? For those interested in the process of cultural dynamism and cultural change, neither the language of rights nor that of culture is likely to prove adequate.

Rights versus justice: Issa Shivji

If Martin Chanock's essay tends to eulogise the language of rights, Issa Shivji's essay begins by interrogating rights through the prism of justice. The journey takes him first to a discussion of group versus individual rights, and then to a notion of group culture that many participants at the conference thought was insufficiently problematised.

While Chanock views rights through the lens of a Western journey, Shivji locates them in an African historical context. Shivji is concerned that the African context has given rise to a dual breach: between rights and justice and, even more so, between democracy and justice. Both are the result of a historical trajectory whereby the state assumed responsibility for the delivery of justice, whereas rights – highlighted as procedural and individual – articulated a demand for freedom against the state. As a result, the language of rights has not only been anti-statist; it has also lacked a potential for articulating the demand for justice. In a context where the state has assumed charge of delivering justice, the practice of justice-from-above has turned out to be undemocratic. It has excluded those directly affected – particularly village communities and disadvantaged groups – from the processes that define the nature and content of justice.

Shivji's essay sums up the point of view of the Tanzanian Land Commission, which he chaired, and is written as a polemic against the point of view advanced by the ODE expatriate who drafted the Land Act that repudiated the central recommendations of the Land Commission. Shivji defines the dilemma as follows: while the Land Commission called for a community-based notion of justice to join the discourse on justice with that on democracy, the draft Land Act sought to build on the statist tradition which is the legacy of both the colonial and the Nyerere years.

The Land Commission departed from the statist tradition in that it recognised the demand for participation as the key grievance of rural communities. 'Hatukushirikishwa' – We were not consulted: so rural respondents told the Commission time and again. The Commission thus recommended that the title and administration of lands in the country be radically diversified between village and national lands, and that village lands be self-administered. Just as radically, the Commission turned upside down the colonial legacy of subordinating customary to received Western law by proclaiming the supremacy of customary law.[2] The reversal was recommended within the context of a double reform that would distinguish customary law from the colonial construct of the same name. Firstly, it was not state-appointed chiefs, but the *wazee* (elders) elected by the community, who would define custom; secondly, while custom so defined would have original jurisdiction in all land matters, it would have to abide by the provision that all household land be owned jointly by men and women cultivating it.

Issa Shivji's essay raises one major question. Why should the *wazee* be the only source of custom and thus of customary law? Why are only the *wazee* recognised as a group, and no other? Why are procedural rights recognised only for individual members of one disadvantaged group – women – and not for others: classes such as poor peasants, age categories such as youth, or social categories such as the disabled? The explanation that the Land Commission assumed – and thus presumably also tried to facilitate – namely, a regime of rich and middle peasant accumulation at the village level, is disarming but does not wholly answer the question. The point is that the Commission needed to think through the question of custom democratically and dynamically. Why are no other sources of custom to be officially recognised and sanctioned?

Was not the key change wrought by colonialism in the sphere of 'customary law' to privilege a single authority – chiefs – as the source of custom, thereby sanctioning an authoritarian version of custom as law? In a context where there had been multiple sources of custom – not only chiefs, but also clans, women's groups, age groups – and no single authoritative source in all social domains, was not the effect to silence every contrary version and expand the authority of the chief to every social domain? The Commission's recommendation replaces the chief by the *wazee,* but it does not recognise alternative sources of custom. In recommending that the *wazee* be elected, it does not recognise contending interests in society and their versions of custom. We return to the question: Why should village elders be the only group to decide the 'principles of justice, fairness and equity held in common by Tanzanian communities'?

One needs to recall Chanock's observation that market relations generate social tensions, particularly around gender and generational relations. What kinds of tensions are likely to be the most fruitful sources of progressive cultural change in contemporary Tanzania? To think through this question requires us to be explicit about the politics of cultural change.

The significance of politics: Kimberle Crenshaw

Kimberle Crenshaw contributes an assessment of the post-Second World War civil rights struggle in the United States. She is interested in seeing how rights performed there in order to understand their possibilities in Africa. Theoretically, she seeks to problematise rights, not through a critique that contrasts the procedural character of abstract rights with the substantive nature of concrete needs, but through a demonstration that it is the very abstract nature of rights that makes for its contradictory effects within real processes. Beginning with the observation that a rights discourse can have a liberating effect at one moment and can facilitate domination at another, she concludes that as outcomes of a single dynamic these contradictory effects cannot be separated. They belong together.

As the good and the bad side of the same process, transformation and legitimisation come in a single package. One does not have the option of choosing between them. On the one hand, the transformation is real, even if partial. On the other, the legitimising potential of rights discourse is possible precisely because of its transforming potential. Without it, legitimisation would appear as nothing but a naked discourse of power. I will suggest that rights talk legitimises power because it develops an *accountability* of power. We shall see that to understand both the possibilities and limits of a discourse on accountability, one needs to distinguish between rights and power.

Crenshaw focuses on the shift in the rights discourse of US courts from a victim's perspective to what she terms a perpetrator's perspective. (I suggest that it is better to think of the shift as being from a victim's perspective to a beneficiary's perspective.) Federal courts took the victim's perspective in the 1960s and 1970s when they placed limitations on traditional rights: white businesses could not exclude patrons simply because of their race (limiting the right of property), whites generally could not refuse to contract with an African American solely on account of race (limiting the right of contract), red-lining and other banking practices were precluded (limiting the unfettered movement of capital), and employers could not use tests and other devices that disproportionately disadvantaged African Americans without giving clearly rational reasons (regulating discretion in employment).

The shift from a victim to a perpetrator model took place in the 1980s. The perpetrator model – requiring that a perpetrator be identified as an active agent behind every unequal outcome – actually camouflaged the beneficiary of unequal historical processes. The courts thus required that a direct link between cause and effect be established in each case for a rights violation to be proved. By highlighting agency and obscuring unequal structured outcomes of historical processes, the courts distinguished the perpetrator from the beneficiary. The scope of redress was also narrowed. The courts no longer targeted race-blind treatment which perpetuated structured outcomes and thus continued to racialise beneficiaries and victims; instead, they targeted only those unequal outcomes which could be directly linked to rights violations. The more structural agnosticism led to a one-sided accent on proving the agency of perpetrators, the more notions of justice shifted from a de-racialising justice to a race-blind justice. The shift had been fourfold: one, a shift in focus from historically structured outcomes to agency-based outcomes; two, a shift from a group-based to an individual definition of the victim; third, a shift from a de-racialising to a race-blind notion of justice; and finally, an overall shift in perspective from that of the victim to that of the beneficiary. For the courts to separate the perpetrator from the beneficiary, so as to highlight the former and obscure the latter, was indeed to take the point of view of the beneficiary.

How did this shift occur? This question takes us from the discourse of rights to the politics of the rights struggle. Crenshaw's answer is that the opportunity for reform was created by a tension within power, specifically between federal and state authorities. The rights discourse inserted itself into this tension. She further argues that the non-democratic nature of federal courts sealed them against angry majorities. Yet, it is clear that this sealing effect was only temporary. Sooner or later, federal courts did begin to reflect the mood of the 'angry majority.'

The rights struggle advanced in the 1960s and 1970s through a combined strategy that involved both their assertion from below and their recognition by the courts from above. How is one to understand what Crenshaw describes as the 'relative failure of the rights struggle as it moved north'? Could it be that the relationship between reform pressures from below and reform initiatives from above became ruptured in a changing landscape? If so, this failure would then need to be understood mainly as a political failure: a failure to reorganise the movement from below in the face of a changing political landscape defined by demobilising reforms from above. That turning point is highlighted by the growing political debate within the rights movement as it approached the turning point – something beyond the scope of Crenshaw's essay.

If the opportune moment for the rights struggle arose with a crisis within power, to what extent did the crisis of the rights movement also correspond to a reorganisation of power? Crenshaw asks whether there is a crisis within the power in Africa that corresponds to the divide between federal and state authorities in the post-war United States. She wonders if the divide between law and religion, or that between law and tradition, could correspond to the American situation. To put the question differently, could culture be the cutting edge of a rights struggle within Africa? This does not mean that Crenshaw ignores the tendency for culture to reify the exercise of power within it. Rather, she notes that this tendency peaks precisely alongside the crisis of that power: thus, power in the South defended itself in the language of culture precisely when it faced a culture of resistance in the South. The point is that the language of culture need not lend itself just to masking power.

It seems to me that the key lesson to be drawn from Crenshaw's analysis is that there is no way to guarantee how a right will be applied in context. She rejects both the standpoint of the critics – who argue that the movement was a victim of false consciousness, not recognising that an accent on rights inevitably deflects from needs because rights are abstract and ahistorical whereas needs are concrete and historical – and that of liberals who believe that African Americans were just as inevitably beneficiaries of an emancipatory world-historical march of rights. Both, she says, deny the agency of African Americans and, in doing so, ignore the importance of politics. The lesson highlights the centrality of politics rather than the theoretical inadequacy of a rights discourse in a struggle for reform.

The politics of reform, I: Nivedita Menon

While a right is stated in the abstract as a principle, no right can be applied in the absolute in practice. This is particularly so because actual contexts often present us with a clash between rights. Once again, we need to turn to the arena of politics to understand how each right is applied and thus limited in practice. Nivedita Menon's paper on the growing differentiation within the women's movement in India highlights just such a context. In this instance, the clash is between two rights, both constitutionally guaranteed: on the one hand, the struggle for equality within the family; on the other, the right of religious communities to their way of life. While the struggle for equality within the family accented the civil rights of women as individuals, religious communities demanded that their way of life be protected as the cultural right of groups. The tension came to a head with the Shah Bano case in 1985: following it, the Hindu religious right decided to cast the struggle for gender rights as one for a uniform civil code in the face of demands by minority, particularly Muslim, communities for separate codes.

In this changing context, it became difficult to think of the struggle for a uniform civil code from a single-issue standpoint. Each organised group within the women's movement was compelled to rethink its position with regard to both the overall objective and the strategy of reform. Should the overall objective continue to be the demand for a uniform civil code, or should it accommodate the need for diversity? Should the strategy be to attain this objective through internal reform and persuasion within communities, or should this be combined with legal reform and thus state compulsion?

Menon points out that it is when the religious right began to line up behind the demand for a uniform code that the democratic movement was compelled to rethink this demand as part of the agenda of an undemocratic majority (Crenshaw's 'angry majority'). The same impetus led to an historical rethink regarding the significance of creating a uniform Hindu Personal Law in the post-independence era. Had not the codification of Hindu Personal Law elevated particular regional, sectional, caste and class practices and turned them into the required norm for all? Those so persuaded now shifted to a call for a 'common' or a 'general' code, implying an outcome that could crystallise a minimal consensus while accommodating differences.

Menon points out that the debate on strategies turned on the questions of statism and democratic reform. For the first few decades after independence, from the 1950s to the mid-1980s, there was apparently a consensus around a statist strategy, that the state be held accountable for ensuring gender justice. Two major tendencies gelled in the aftermath of the Shah Bano case. One called for a compulsory and uniform code, to be enforced from above by law. The other called for a voluntary code, allowing for difference and diversity, arrived at through internal reform from below.

Between these, there were various combinations. I have identified at least four strategies of incremental reform ranging from (a) an exclusive reliance on internal reform forces; to (b) combining an internal reform with a legally enforced reform in those marginal areas, such as domestic violence and economic rights, which lie outside the jurisdiction of personal law; to (c) an internal reform process facilitated and spurred on by state-enforced minimum rights; to (d) giving women the choice of opting out of the system by creating a code of gender-just personal laws parallel to religious personal laws.

Besides mapping the variety of gender-focused groups in India, Menon brings to light theoretical issues that have been at the heart of the debate on gender. The first concerns the question of community. The debate on community has led to a growing consensus that there is nothing primordial about community. Most participants agree that all communities are historical creations. The difference lies in whether the religious or caste communities are wholly a colonial construct (Chakravarthy) or whether their construction involved several agencies, not only the colonial state but also particular interests within the communities that came to be (Bayly).

I am tempted to add a further question. Even if the communities in question were wholly constructed by the colonial state, did not the very outcome unleash the agency of particular sections and muffle that of others? Does not the history of personal law and its construction in the nineteenth and twentieth centuries testify to this? From this point of view, it would seem to be important to ask questions such as: when the constitution guarantees communities their 'way of life' (custom), who in the community is to determine this way of life? We return to the question posed in relation to Issa Shivji's contribution to land law: given an ongoing struggle around the definition of the 'customary', what kind of reform can give maximum play to this struggle and, thereby, to those forces with the greatest stake in a gender-just reform of personal laws from within?

Like Crenshaw's discussion of the civil rights movement, Menon's essay also brings a series of tensions to the fore. How is one to theorise a series of changes, such as those in the relationship between pressures from below and reform from above; or in the shift from a focus on civil–political rights against the state to social–economic rights to be realised through the state; or in the tension between the original feminist critique of the family and the concrete struggle for rights within the family which must tend to strengthen the family the more it succeeds; or in the contradiction between the abstract demand for equal rights which risks treating women as if they were men (and, one might add, Muslims as if they were Hindus) and, in the process, disadvantaging them at points where they are indeed different, and the reality-based call for a differential treatment which risks ending up with discrimination and the pious hope that separate can indeed be equal? Whether it relates to the contradiction between democracy and statism, reform and transformation, or sameness and difference, it seems worthwhile recalling Crenshaw's observation that there is no way to guarantee how a right will be applied in context. If this is so, then these tension-filled relationships cannot be theorised and 'fixed' regardless of context. Each needs to be resolved afresh, in practice, through a concrete and dynamic political analysis.

The politics of reform, II: Hussaina Abdullah

The contradictory nature of the reform process is brought out in Hussaina Abdullah's essay on the diversity of feminist politics in Nigeria. Just as the forces of the religious Hindu right in India reached out to women to control an expanding political arena, so did non-progressive forces in Nigeria – particularly the army – facilitate, and even organise, the participation of women so as to control it. The result was an explosion of different kinds of feminism: state feminism alongside civil society feminism, legal feminism alongside radical feminism, and secular feminism alongside religious feminism. Abdullah's essay allows us to glimpse concretely an instance where religion, too, operates not just as a language of domination, but also as an idiom through which to battle for reforms.

The Nigerian experience also clarifies the relationship between rights and power. Except for the radical organisation called WIN, none of the reform tendencies in the landscape that Abdullah sketches claims to be anti-power. Each is able to take advantage of tensions within power to find space for a struggle for reforms. Rather than challenging power, most actually pay homage to it. Secular feminists in civil society such as those of FIDA, draw a clear distinction between civil and political society, and rights and power: they want equal rights, which they distinguish from any challenge to power. State feminists seek to expand women's participation in the public sphere through diverse mobilisations, whether ethnic or religious; in the process, they both seek to reform the state and tend to incorporate women's agency within a state-defined political orbit. Religious feminists in civil society, such as those in FOMWAN, make a distinction between Islamic principles and their historical application. By historicising Islamic practice, they critique it. They affirm their allegiance to the principles of the Quran but question its changing application in the Hadith or Sharia as falling short of the original promise. In the process, they seek to reform Islamic practice while incorporating the agency of reform within Islam.

Each of the Nigerian feminist tendencies – and I will come to the exception – combines a strategy of internal reform from below with a call for legal reform from above. They illustrate in practice the contradictory character of reform movements. The only exception – according to Abdullah's account – is the case of WIN. But this exception, too, seems to make the same point: WIN seems more educational than mobilisational in its thrust; when it does seek to mobilise, its impetus is more agitational than organisational. Its radicalism has more to do with its single-minded focus on the absolute character of rights as principles than with a struggle for their qualified and conditional application in practice. Her eye very much on the need for ongoing reform, Abdullah closes the chapter with a double call: for a minimum-action programme for today, and for a far-reaching rights-based agenda to provide the basis for continuing agitation tomorrow.

Abdullah's analysis of the Nigerian case presents us with a double irony. On the one hand, it is the military more than any other force which has ushered women into the public sphere; on the other, the expanded entry of women into the public sphere has gone alongside an expansion – and not contraction – of ethnic and religious mobilisation. The contradictory development must have a sobering effect on those nurtured by an *a priori* optimism that sees the participation of the 'wretched of the earth' in the public arena as necessarily emancipatory in its effect.

Religion in the public sphere: Moosa

Ebrahim Moosa's concern is the relationship between religion and the state as defined in the post-apartheid South African Constitution. If the post-apartheid legal and political order shows every sign of being an imported turnkey project, then religion needs to be seen as part of a local and indigenous socio-cultural order. The discussion allows him to rethink the question of secularism from the standpoint of a religious minority rather than that of an anti-religious polemic.

The Christian church in South Africa has played a pivotal role in framing the terms of the post-apartheid transition. Rather than leaving the public sphere, it has defined for itself an activist role in engagement with the new power. This point of view was first formulated in the Declaration issued by the 1992 Inter-Faith Conference of the South African Chapter of the World Conference on Religion and Peace (WCRP). While pledging submission to the rule of law, the church foresaw an active political role for itself. Somewhat naïvely, it hoped that any conflict between religion and the state would be resolved through dialogue rather than confrontation. The 1996 Constitution and the Bill of Rights, too, define a public role for religion. The law permits religion in the public sphere, provided access is free, voluntary and equitable. It recognises the possibility of religious personal law. Most importantly, there is no Jeffersonian wall of separation between church and state.

Moosa's critique of the relationship between religion and the state in the 1996 Constitution has three parts to it. Moosa's first observation is that legal regulation does not reflect actual religious diversity in the country. On the one hand, rights talk lacks a local rootedness, an indigenous cultural foundation: unlike in the Preamble to the 1993 Constitution, there is no reference to an indigenous principle like *ubuntu*. The lack of an *indigenous* foundation is not, however, the same as the lack of a *local* foundation, for, as Moosa points out, the turnkey character of the Constitution reflects the hegemonic position of important local minorities which hold cultural allegiance to the West.

Moosa's second observation concerns the absence of a wall of separation between church and state. The result, he says, is that religion in South Africa is more vulnerable to legislative and judicial interference than it is in the United States. One is tempted to say that this is an inevitable trade-off: if one wants a public role for religion, one has to accept the risk of state interference in religious affairs. From this point of view, one wonders whether the more important consequence of the absence of a wall of separation between church and state has been precisely to reinforce the position of the religious minority wedded to a rights culture.

The final reflection concerns the tension between the absolute guarantee of religion as belief and the practice of religion as limited by the secular constitution. As several contributions to this volume show, such a tension is inevitable in any democratic set-up. No right can be absolute in practice. Every right has to be realised contextually, in tension with other rights and the rights of others. Moosa recognises that legal history evolves in the gap between principle and practice. The tension between the two defines the realm of possibilities. It is this realm which belongs to the domain of politics.

The changing application of rights means that there is no way of fixing a boundary between law and politics, no way of defining *a priori* what is a legal issue and what a political issue. The shift in the way legislatures define politics and the way the courts define rights shows that the line between politics and law is ever-changing. Legal principles are stubborn to change, and yet their application in practice is variable. Not only the medium-term shift in principles, but also the varying gap between principle and practice in the short run, is politically driven. The moral of the story is that it takes political action to create legal space for progressive social change.

Chapter One

'Culture' and human rights: orientalising, occidentalising and authenticity

Martin Chanock

Rights and culture

This essay is an effort to unravel the discourses around the question of 'culture' and the connections between current modes of explaining the world and the end of the Cold War and the current distribution of power. A number of new narrative paradigms – the New World Order; the End of History; the Clash of Civilisations – have recently appeared as we try to come to grips with explaining the present to ourselves and working up new narratives to project into the future. The collapse of Marxism and the development of theorising about an era of globalisation have naturalised 'culture' as a vital node of explanation.

It is always hard to contextualise our own ways of thinking but we should be clear at least that there is a close association between power and explanation. In this context it would be well to recall the long co-existence of empire with race as the node around which much of the social sciences and explanations of human differences, intelligence, social organisation and capacity for self-government revolved. For a long time race and theories of racial difference held a central place in 'realistic' explanations in the West,[1] and political and scientific analysis turned around race. It is almost too easy to contextualise such thinking and its connection with empire now, but harder to come to grips accurately with the connections in the present between the ways in which power is distributed in the world and the growing centrality of culture as an explanatory tool. In essence the suggestion in this essay is that those rights discourses in which culture is invoked as an argument against universalism now largely belong to rulers, not to those who may need rights protected, who talk in terms of wrongs and needs, not rights and culture.[2]

Rights, culture and religion

This section will remind us of some basic elements of the history of rights in the West which have been overshadowed during the Cold War, during which Western propaganda presented rights as inherent in a particular path of historical evolution and progress. It points to certain features of the history of rights: that the entrenching of rights in politics and law typically do not have their origins in processes of cultural evolution but have come about as the result of major conflicts and sharp breaks with the past; that conceptualisations of rights have necessarily been universalist in nature; and that they have been inextricably linked to the triumph of secularism in the state and the breaking of the hold of religious orthodoxy on public institutions.

The major rights declarations have had what Preuss has called 'catastrophic origins' (Orwell & Rosenfeld 1994: 150). The English Bill of Rights, the American Bill of Rights and the French Declaration of the Rights of Man all arose from civil war, war for independence or revolution. Each reflects a revolt against specific oppressions, specific wrongs. The Universal Declaration of the Rights of Man followed the worst of global wars. More recently, the new rights-based constitutional orders ushered in by the West German Constitution, and later by the post-communist regimes of Eastern Europe, both depended on a dramatic break with the practices, and the legal and political cultures, of the previous regimes – a denial of the immediate political and legal past – not on an evolutionary process. Indeed it was the sharpness of the break which established the legitimacy of the new rights-based legal order, which was based on imported political and legal models. The same was the case with the new South African Constitution. Disjunction, in other words, rather than continuity has given birth to rights.

It is not easy to combine with this a cultural view of rights which implies that a consensus about rights is deeply embedded in, and reflective of, cultures. Rights would seem to belong to the disputed realm of politics rather than to a deeper expressive realm of culture. Human rights have depended on the deliberate (bitterly opposed) active remaking of a new order, on a denial of the past, on a reinvention of political mythologies, not simply on an evolution of what had been historically and culturally acceptable. In doing this, the rights makers have specifically reached out towards universalism, and very often explicitly away from 'culture' in a more specific sense. Rights may be claimed by their proponents as an inherent immanent virtue but they do not simply emerge and they do not proclaim compatibility with what 'is' in a culture. They come from the fiercest of political contestation, from revolution and from war, and depend thereafter very much on artificial legal formulations with almost infinitely variable wordings and meanings. (The protracted debates about how to word particular rights in Bills of Rights, and the endless and convoluted legal debates as to how they should be interpreted, should make this clear.)

It is with this notion of catastrophic origins that we should be approaching the history of rights in the contemporary world. The past five decades have seen the end of European empires and the intense political struggles between those who wished to establish alternative regimes of power over much of the globe. These struggles have taken place first in the context of the Cold War, and now in the context of the new and disruptive processes known as globalisation. War, internal violence and political repression, and not an immanent progress towards rights, have dominated recent political history.

It is also very clear from the history of 'rights' in Western political cultures that they were established as a part of the struggle between political rights and religion and that they have been a part of the conquest of the power of institutionalised religion in the state. In both the French and American cases the rights-based state came with (and has continued to be associated with) the firm separation of church and state. Rights, then, are a product of a continuing secularisation of political institutions, not a product of accommodation with religious power in the state. While they have clearly co-existed with the continuation of strong religious cultures, they have been established as a part of law and politics when state and church have been separated by political struggle. It is notable that Western political theorising on the basis of state and society boils down to what Preuss has termed 'blood or contract' – a shared racial and ethnic kinship, or a social contract, as the basis of citizenship and community. Absent from the theorising of the modern state has been 'belief' as an organising basis of society. Western political, legal and constitutional thought is fundamentally secular.

The absence for so long of 'belief' as part of what is discursively legitimate in Western constitutional traditions is, therefore, more than fashion or oversight; it is built into the nature of constitutionalism (and concomitantly of rights discourses) itself. Current post-communist political discourses turn around the polarities of state and market, and the identification of the former with coercion and the latter with consent. Within these polarities, as within the realms of public and private, Western institutions, law, theorising and practices have now placed religion within the realm of the private and the consensual. Neither the discourses nor the institutions of Western constitutionalism appear to permit a relocation of religion into the public and coercive realm.

International rights standards and the African case: the nature of culture

The primary problem is to identify what is meant by culture, the times at which the notion of culture is invoked, and the uses to which this invocation is put.

Many of the problems posed by these questions result from a tendency to posit a concept of cultures as unities, and therefore easily distinguishable from and opposable to each other. After centuries of imperialism, and in the current period of high-velocity cultural globalisation, this is a fantasy. There are no longer (if ever there were) single cultures in any country/polity/legal system, but many. Cultures are very complex conversations within any social formation. The concept of culture has become a prime way of describing groups and is displacing other primary labels like race, class, gender or nationality at a particular time and in particular circumstances. How and when culture assumed this importance in describing group difference and political affiliation should therefore be our framing question. We may note that it is a departure from the universalism implicit in class analysis, in which the worker has no country. And it is also a departure from the differentiating idea of nation. The cultural rejection of universal rights is now not based on *national* differences but assumes that above and beyond national distinctiveness (based on language, place, historical association and narrative, and so on) there is something larger – European, Asian, African; or Christian, Muslim, Confucian – which distinguishes people from each other. The first of these looks suspiciously like a different way of talking about racial differences, while the second not just invokes broad differences in 'civilisations' but links them to the possession of religious truths. Why our discourses have passed from class and nation to this kind of analysis is a question of some importance. It could be said that it is a part of the development of a global narrative in a post-nation-state, post-Cold War world – as evidenced by the 'clash of civilisations' thesis. But culture has also developed not just as a way of substituting larger aggregations for nation and class, but also as a way of distinguishing very small groups from each other. While 'nation' and 'class' seem to be dying as explanatory categories for conflict and difference, larger 'civilisations' and smaller ethnic groups have come to life as legitimate aggregations.

The African case illustrates specifically how the evolving relationship between using race as the way to describe difference, and using culture to perform the same task, is a part of the intellectual history of empire. Even while the earlier social sciences were freeing themselves from racially determined explanations of difference, they remained within a broad narrative of cultural evolution in which there were backward cultures (which could, if guided, move forward). Cultural difference, like racial difference, was a marker of inferiority and condemnation. The practical experiences of colonial rule, and the development of the anthropology of African societies, produced changes in this paradigm. African cultures were subject to a variety of portrayals, from exotic, to different but functionally equal, to functionally necessary so as to prevent social disintegration. For a variety of reasons both Western governors and social scientists came to defend cultural differences) Likewise, African intellectuals abandoned an early acceptance of cultural assimilation, and celebrated, elaborated and defended difference. The point being laboured is simple, that discursive deployment of culture takes place within particular histories of political and intellectual power and in each has had its particular usages and meanings. Therefore, if we are now using culture as an important variable we must seriously analyse the context, reasons and meanings of its deployment. Clearly also, this is not just a matter of intellectual discourses but also of popular experiences. How and when do people experience having a cultural identity, rather than a class or national one? What can the defence of cultural authenticity mean in a world in which the conditions of symbolic production and exchange are being so dramatically altered?

The leaders (and their defenders) of those states in Africa and Asia which do not meet the standards laid down in the various international declarations of rights frequently make the claim that the rights enumerated are cultural, and are part of alien, formerly dominant cultures, rather than universal. They are clearly correct if the claim is seen as a recognition that these rights, and the ways in which they are described (and institutionalised), arise out of particular historical experiences in Western Europe and America and that they are part of a constantly worked-over narrative of the legal and political cultures of some of these countries. They were also originally 'universal' only rhetorically and they could co-exist without much discomfort not only with both empire and slavery, but with the effective denial of the universal rights to an 'internal' majority.

But the claim that 'rights' are cultural does not dispose of the question of the desirability of 'rights' being universal. There is little reason why the currently dominant versions of 'culture' in parts of Africa or Asia should remain unchanged and unchallenged. They could as well be subjected to precisely the kind of cultural work that transformed a rhetoric of rights in the West applicable only to property-owning white men into one which eventually spread to encompass in form, and slowly but increasingly in practice, all persons regardless of colour or gender. The achievement of both colour and gender equality in the West required and still requires a transformation of the cultures of many institutions – workplaces, trade unions, the church, the legal profession, families, political parties, schools and so on – all at a different rate and in different ways. Gender equality, for example, could just as well have been described as alien to Western cultures as to non-Western ones. Certainly it was (and continues in important aspects to be) rejected by major Christian churches. It is the product of intense political struggle and cultural work, not immanence.

One might wonder also just how much the current state of lack of rights in Africa and Asia has anything to do with African and Asian cultures at all. Certainly the major abuses of political rights at the state level are the products of the political institutions bequeathed by the colonial powers; of their weaknesses, and failures to deal with the multi-ethnic states created by colonialism; and of their powerlessness in relation to the goals of development because of the structure and workings of the world economy. Why anyone outside of the small elite which has benefited from this state of affairs would want to defend it as culturally 'African' is not clear. On the other hand, there are features of post-colonial African 'cultures' which do not conform to the universalised version of rights rhetoric, particularly in relation to gender discrimination in property ownership and marriage. Should these be protected, on the grounds of cultural inviolability, from the kinds of political and cultural struggles over property and gender which have been, and are, a feature of Western politics?

Much of the international debate about 'culture' and rights concerns gender, a field in which mutual occidentalising and orientalising has been long established (Nader 1989). It is essentially only in the last few decades that a wide gap has opened between 'West' and 'non-West' on the issue of gender equality. Gender inequality is, as I have already noted, as much a part of the 'culture' of the 'West' as of other 'cultures'. What needs to be explored is the reasons for the rapidity of changes in one part of the world though not in others; but this is not an exploration which is either useful or necessary for those engaged in cultural representations, either to defend or to criticise them. This issue might usefully be considered in our context in relation to sexual behaviour, the rules governing the permissible and impermissible, and the long history of inter-cultural representations of sexuality. Judgements about the sexual behaviour of the people colonised by Europe played a core part in cultural othering and were central to the representation of the 'horror', to use Kurtz's term, that was seen. In the early judgements of the West on matters like harems, *lobolo* and Hindu art, promiscuity was perceived to be at the core of other cultures. Now this same judgement is being made in the other direction. This should at least alert us towards its role in cultural othering. Gender equality is linked, by the spokesmen of, for example, Islamic cultures, to promiscuity in the West, as a twinned pair of horrors in an othered sexual culture. The power of this cultural imagery stands in the way of movement on each specific legal gender inequality.

Much of the essentialising of the notion of culture, in the past few decades of rapid change in Africa, has been done in the context of the confrontational dialogues between generations and genders. These confrontations became particularly acute in times of change associated not simply with acculturation to 'foreign' ideas, but with fundamental economic and social changes which accompanied the introduction of the money economy, migrant labour, urbanisation and pressures on forms of land tenure. The entrenchment of the 'cultural' response to change in Africa owes much as well to the attitude of both colonial and successor governments towards economic and social change. Colonial governments wanted to minimise the 'cultural' effects of economic changes because of an overriding fear of instability, and a similar stance – the view of change as disintegration – has been evident in successor independent governments. Culture was employed as a defence for, justification of and positioning for advantage in a field of conflict over resources, as well as being invoked as a metaphor for handling and resisting huge changes in ways of living. It has also been employed as a metaphor around which generations and genders, otherwise sharply divided, could be encouraged to unite in opposition to outsiders.

It is relatively easy to trace these processes in the history of Africa in the twentieth century. The challenge in the present is to realise that it is processes of this sort, in late-twentieth-century guise, which continue to give rise to invocations of culture, and not the 'existence' of unified 'cultures'. It is internal conflict about ways of doing things, far more than any conflict with outsiders, that has led to the essentialising of cultures. Pragmatic practices become 'customs' to be insisted on; styles of religious practice become beliefs and orthodoxies. The intensity of some of the feelings of cultural belonging, and strength of attachment to custom, are testimony of the seriousness of the conflicts and the pace of displacement and change. The elite controllers of institutions (perhaps most importantly, state education systems), and of symbols, can resist internal generational, gender and other challenges by the deployment of images of an essentialised culture under external challenge. 'Authenticity', and a consequent cultural patriotism, become a routinised response to globalisation. Such essentialising responses to change are ways of exerting authority, and they display partial immunity to discursive challenge, especially if it comes from an external source, as such challenge frequently serves to strengthen convictions.

Cultural differences are not simply given. The experience of difference depends on the power to create culture, on the labour of elites in essentialising, displaying, and institutionalising elements of the myriad of practices in any community. Our focus should therefore be on the current processes of cultural creation. The processes of creation and representation of cultures in the post-colonial and post-Cold War world form one of multiple and mutual intersections between the elites of West and non-West.[3] While the continuing process of 'orientalising' has been much complained of by the orientalised, the elites of the 'orientalised' cultures of the world have been actively complicit both in their own representation of themselves as 'other' and in the reverse process of occidentalising, in which the 'West', and especially individuality in Western cultures, is symbolised and portrayed as an opposing essence to the communality of the cultures that non-Western intellectuals (religious and secular) represent and control. Indeed, the establishment of this difference between individualism and communalism is crucial to the non-

Western elites' claim to constitute and to lead their 'cultures'. It has become increasingly vociferous precisely because globalised communications, public cultures, rights and constitutionalism have all meant that the claims of local elites are more fiercely resisted and contested within their own 'homes'.

There has been far less interest in the intellectual process of occidentalising than there has been in orientalising.[4] The former has taken two basic forms. One is the habit of Western scholars of non-Western societies in having resort to unexamined clichés concerning an undifferentiated 'West'. As Carrier notes of this imagined entity, 'The occidentalised West is an imagined entity that, in its memorable clarity, obscures the vast areas of Western life that conflict with its vision ...' (1995: 28). The second is the process by which the intellectuals in non-Western societies construct identities in opposition to imagined features of the 'West'. Both draw consciously on the major dichotomy of the grand narrative of Western history – that of *gemeinschaft* and *gesellschaft* – but allocate cohesive Community to the non-West, and atomised Society to the West. An historical transition from agricultural to industrial societies is thereby transmuted into an a-historical cultural divide. New value judgements have become a part of this essentialising. Carrier observes how non-Western societies are typified by 'generosity, peace and dignity' and inhabited by 'wise ecologist(s) attuned to a fragile nature', while the West is 'violent, rapacious and heedless' (ibid.: 10). There is a search, writes Spencer, for essences, cores or central cultural symbols where differences between cultures seem to 'hover on the edge of absolute incommensurability' (ibid.: 242).

Just as orientalising was a part of imperialism and colonialism, so occidentalising is a part of the emergence from colonial rule and cultural power. The West is used, Spencer writes, as a 'rhetorical counter'; occidentalism is a 'mnemonic for the cultural contradictions engendered by colonial domination' (ibid.: 236). Images of the West are deployed as part of a 'rhetoric of authenticity' (ibid.: 236), which opposes itself to Western modes of thought and cultural institutions and practices. This is, frequently, a positive process. Spencer writes, 'Other people's essentialisms are ... often crucial components in attempts to re-imagine or re-build forms of community and solidarity which they feel are needed to deal with the West ...' (ibid.: 250). Historical dichotomies, as he points out, can be used to illustrate widely differing political positions; '... the village community of the East was once used as a kind of political Rorschach from which all observers could draw their own conclusions' (ibid.: 246).

The deployment of the dichotomy between those cultures which emphasise individuals or individualism and those cultures which emphasise the 'group' (so common a part of the 'dialogue' about rights between the West and some Asian countries) has a long history. The critique of so-called individualism had particular strength in socialist attacks on capitalism in the late nineteenth century. These European debates spilled over into analyses of other cultures. As Kidd's book *Kafir Socialism* (1908) shows, in reverse mode, description of the communal aspects of African life could be used as a condemnation and marker of cultural inferiority, and the suggestion that Africans were communal was used as an argument that this was a mode of social organisation of primitives, and obviously not meant for progressive Europeans.[5] The terms of this argument, as well as the drawing-in of non-European cultures, were deployed in one sense in the struggle between right and left at the end of the nineteenth century, and in the opposite sense during the Cold War. In the 1960s African Socialism was linked by its protagonists to all that was progressive in universal history, ahead of the outdated individualism of the West. It is this critical attitude towards individualism that remains in the non-Western world even though its universalist partner, socialism, lacks contemporary credibility. Reflections on the nature of these discursive deployments should at least make us aware that when the terms are used it is not only for purposes of description or analysis. The complex history of the opposition of the representations has been more about marking difference than about substance.

The long tradition of liberal philosophies of rights, as well as Western-inspired rights declarations, is very clearly about groups. They are about the nature of group life, and how it should ideally work. They endeavour to prescribe the ground rules for associating in groups. The differences, therefore, are about the ground rules for associating in groups, not about individuals as opposed to groups, nor even about which has priority. Classical liberalism, from which rights doctrines flow, does not subordinate group to individual, but is concerned with the kind of group to which individuals belong. Furthermore, the attempt to depict Western societies as individualistic misses the point that these very societies, with their powerful cohesive ideologies of nationalism, patriotism, collective action and welfarism, have been and are far more 'successful' groups on a larger scale over long periods of time, with better working consensual traditions of government, than the often fragmented, authoritarian, familial, localistically based societies which invoke their cultural attachment to groupness.[6]

Culture / rights and brands: twinned discourses?

My recourse to literature on advertising came about first from an interest in the more conventional socio-legal questions regarding the regulation of political advertising and the notion of commercial free speech. A passing acquaintance has led me to explore the issues raised in writing about advertising in relation to human rights discourses. Like human rights discourse, advertising discourse is deeply involved in questions of culture and cultural essences. The cultural branding which is involved in orientalising and occidentalising involves similar discursive strategies to those which are central to globalised advertising. The issue of universalism as opposed to cultural particularism is a feature of international advertising analysis, and the notion of the 'brand', with its emphasis on creating an attachment, may well be a way into an analysis of the processes of creating cultures in the post-colonial world. Like human rights discourses, advertising is now a fundamental feature of globalised communications, and the analysis of advertising, the primary globalised discourse, seems to offer possibilities for thinking about globalised rights discourses because globalised advertising confronts, penetrates and uses national and regional cultures as do discourses about rights. Finally, it is becoming harder to continue to separate the issues surrounding the discourses in the public sphere – those relating to law and government – from those in the commercial. It is clear that these are becoming increasingly alike, with the growth of advertising as a primary means by which government communicates, and political persuasion of all sorts is conducted, as well as the claims that commercial speech (in the form of advertisements) is entitled to the same protections accorded to 'political' and 'cultural' speech.

Analysis of the methods of advertising, in particular the core process of creating brands, may well yield insights into the selling of cultures by intellectual entrepreneurs in the post-colonial world. The longstanding analyses of culture relate it to social structure, to behaviours predicated upon that structure, to the world of materiality and action from which are derived the intellectual constructs that explain and interpret the society to itself and others. In a world of globalised communications and representations, these links between structure, behaviour and cultural representation can no longer be taken for granted. As Daniel Boorstin asked, 'How do the expressions of our peculiar folk culture come to us? They no longer spring from the earth, from the village, from the farm, or even from the neighbourhood or the city.' They come, he said, from centralised sources, 'from advertising agencies, from networks of newspapers, from radio and television' (Mattelart 1991: 32). These different ingredients, if now taken into account, should suggest to us that culture may be analysed without giving primacy to social structure.[7] The disjunction of representation from reality, and the power of unreal representations to create behaviours, give a different chicken-and-egg sequence to the explanation of cultures.

Another basic feature of analyses of culture is that they are based on the assumption that the realm of culture is one of relative permanence and stability and temporal depth. Cultures are seen as being developed over long periods in relatively closed and stable communities which generate shared patterns of behaviour and belief that are comprehensible, communicable and legitimate to members of a group over prolonged periods of time. While not static, they retain sufficient 'core' to remain recognisably differentiated from other cultures. But this form of analysis, while it may once have been appropriate to explain the long-term development of nationalism and national cultures, or the practices and beliefs of isolated communities, may no longer be appropriate to a world of glob-alised communications in which the circulation of knowledge and images has been dramatically increased in volume and speed. In Mattelart's words, there is a contest between 'globalised industrial cultural production and individual cul-tures', in a world in which, through advertising, 'a permanent, daily and gener-alised connection is developed between particular societies and cultures, local, regional and national' (ibid.: 216, 231). This is not an argument which neces-sarily leads towards global homogeneity of cultures (for the existence of new stimuli may accelerate the production of differences), simply one which suggests that the circumstances of cultural formation are now significantly different, and that temporal depth and relative continuities of practice and belief may no longer be at the heart of a concept of 'culture'.

All of this is well known to students of media, communications and popular culture, but is curiously absent from the notions of 'culture' used in the human rights debates, in which a sacralised idea of culture still dominates. Another relat-ed issue is that of 'lifestyle'. Year after year my students have wondered why I have objected so strongly to the use of the phrase 'the peasant lifestyle', for today's students do not differentiate between culture, economics and consumer choice. And to a growing extent there is a blurring of the lines between culture and custom, and chosen style. "'The social classes are dead. Long live lifestyles" is the motto of the lifestyle professionals' (ibid.: 167). This is still not to suggest that such choices are universally available, but to indicate that there are other ways of making identities. Mattelart quotes Wolfgang Haug:

> Commodity aesthetics organises imaginary spaces around the commodity … [which] offer the addressee the promise that after purchase, they will reflect in his new self-representation, and … will solve the problem of iden-tity. The imaginary spaces around the product are intended to become spaces in our imagination that will be filled through aesthetic-symbolic activity … consumption induces an imagination of identity. (ibid.: 202)

In inducing this imagination of identity, successful advertising campaigns draw upon deep 'cultural' motifs. As has been frequently pointed out, the 'Marlboro Man' depended on the significance of the '(American) West' in popular culture, as much as he exploited it (ibid.: 53). Mattelart writes of the techniques used to develop (and sell) popular fiction and TV series by legitimising pleasure through the use of 'indicators of authenticity', through the 'promotion of verisimilitude' by the use of historical references and historical culture (ibid.: 136). One can see a parallel in which the promoters of all cultural versions of rights 'use' the past as a way of lending verisimilitude to their versions.

While most public discourses, which are controlled by national elites, emphasise continuing differences, the discourses of the international marketplace tend towards universalising patterns of consumption and behaviour. But while certain images (like the Nike logo) are easily universalised, marketers have found that different cultures require that brands be promoted in different ways. The international market, then, does not make cultures disappear, but it manipulates them in particular ways, using cultural essences to create loyalty to the universal brand. The cultural element is important because it is the manipulation of identity that creates the attachment, which is not based on utility. As advertising agency Saatchi and Saatchi say, 'The relationship that consumers enjoy with a brand is ... a complex mixture of rational and emotional factors ... There are many categories where the emotional relationship ... is ... more important than the functional relationship ...' (1984 report, quoted in Mattelart 1991: 163).

Cook describes the advertising for Bacardi, which features slim young men and women swimming in blue water and lying on a tropical sunlit beach. He comments on what he calls the 'extraordinary reversal': 'Drinking spirits makes people fatter, less fit, less sexually potent and poorer; in direct sunlight it gives people headaches; it is not typically the activity of muscular young men or slim young women in cutaway swimwear, but rather of fat, stressed, middle aged men in suits' (ibid.: 18). Yet these 'reversed' fantasy advertisements were hugely successful in establishing the brand. Fantasies work where reality fails. We must transfer this thought to the way in which we think about cultures. In spite of the retreat of materialism and structuralism, the assumption remains that cultural representations reflect actual social practices. We might try and see if our understanding is enhanced by a consideration of cultures as sustained social imagination, fed in part by imagined versions of other 'cultures' – that is, by the process of orientalisation and occidentalisation. These fantasies, like the Bacardi fantasy, depend on establishing links between aspirations and a brand. The process of branding may, therefore, be full of clues to the understanding of how allegiances to cultures are made. Cultures, like brands, must essentialise, and successful and sustainable cultures are those which brand best.

How far are the usual forms of public communication essentially different from those of advertising? If we assume that they once were different, are they now converging? And, if they are, why now? And what can rights / culture discourses tell us about this convergence? It is becoming harder to continue to accept the view that a clear distinction can ultimately be made between reason and manipulation in public discourses. In particular, in relation to 'culture' 'commoditised space has become so pervasive that it becomes impossible to continue thinking of culture as a reserved and uncontaminated terrain' (Mattelart 1991: 216). George Orwell's *Animal Farm* and *1984*, and the essays on 'Politics and the English Language', were all based on the absolute premise that behind the corrupted political discourses and language use lay a real truth and a clear way of expressing it. Whether we can meaningfully work with this paradigm in the area of rights discourses seems to me to be increasingly doubtful. For they appear to have more in common with the language and techniques of advertising behind which no truths lie. Design, logo, symbol and packaging (see ibid.: 210) are a part of the world of rights and cultures as they are a part of the basic techniques of advertisements. Indeed, pronouncements about rights often appear to be like the huge hoardings in third world cities which advertise luxury products to people who will never be able to purchase them, as part of the creation of the illusion that they are in some way a part of the life of everyone.[8] We can at least wonder whether the rights that are proclaimed in universal declarations and bills of rights are a luxury product, a product at all, or an advertisement. We know that the media can be mixed: a cigarette can be 'the taste of freedom' (The *L and M* campaign in Eastern Europe: *The Australian*, 28 April 1998). What can freedom be the taste of?

Cultures, of course, have always branded themselves through art and ritual but verbal discourses internal to a culture have, in the past, not tended to perform a branding function. However, as cultures increasingly are thrown together and interleaved in globalised symbolic exchanges, verbal branding of cultural essences tends towards the nature of visual branding – towards art or image. But even bearing these things in mind, can it possibly be correct to situate the ways in which we talk and write about people's greatest needs, most severe oppressions, and most vital aspirations – which is what rights discourses are nominally about – in these terms? It is in particular formerly oppressed and colonised cultures which demand that their own historical experiences and cultural differences be respected, and it is this demand for parity of respect which underpins the stress on the preservation of cultural differentiation, the 'invention of tradition' and the 'imagining of communities'. The need to fight for recognition of different historical experiences, as 'reflected' in different 'cultures', is even greater for the most vulnerable of indigenous communities, as well as for established non-Western societies, in a world in which English is the global language, and in which Western images dominate global commerce. If one suggests that what is happening is to be likened to the process of 'branding', the danger is that one is contributing to a weakening of just claims for recognition, respect, and resources. Should we not rather acknowledge

Bourdieu's view of culture as a kind of 'self-defence' against 'ideological pressure … against abuses of symbolic power directed against them, be they advertising, political propaganda or religious fanaticism' (quoted in Mattelart 1991: 216)? But the price of conceding this kind of cultural essentialism is that one may render people captive to indigenous elites.

These questions have a long discursive history through the colonial period which revolved around issues of 'authenticity'. The dominant model, as Indians, Africans and others came into contact with 'the West', was that these people were rather ridiculous, essentially culturally other, yet assuming a comic and inappropriate veneer of Western civilisation. This model of acculturation had a political purpose, but analytically it failed completely as a means of understanding the nature of the negotiation between different social and symbolic worlds. However, the fallacious notion of 'authenticity' around which this explanation was built survives, indeed is embraced by, the culturalist discourses of the present. It is equally useless in explanation. What this section might suggest is that for many people now a veneer of symbolic cultural 'authenticity' lies over people who are becoming part of an increasingly universalised economy of labour, consumption and imagination. This is not to suggest that this world is uniform at all, but that it, rather than cultural authenticity, is where analysis must start.

Africa: state, market, rights and culture

In the years when colonialism was coming to an end, and nation-states were being established, much of Western scholarship concerned with Africa looked at Africa's prospects (and practices) with a markedly sympathetic eye. Freedom, modernisation and development were all goals and processes which were promised in the new era and there was little doubt displayed that the state was to be the main vector of all of these desirable developments. Now Western scholarship sees the African states through a miasma of failed promises, disappointments and disasters, and the result is suspicion and condemnation. There were two common early models of the African state. In the first the state was the vehicle through which modernisation and development would be developed. In the later, post-Cold War view the state was a guarantor of 'rights', a holder of the ring, while a private economy would deliver development. In both views, the state was seen as essentially politically neutral in a process in which all would benefit.

Whitaker describes the expectation in the early years of independence of a culturally African yet Keynesian polity, a specifically African democracy with Keynesian (or African socialist) management of the development process, in which the elites were to be midwives of development (Sklar and Whitaker 1991:

333ff). Analysts constructed a picture of an African state innocent of class con-flict, though bedevilled by ethnic conflict ('tribalism' – which was Bad Culture), which development would supersede. It took time for the view of the state as something violent, dominant and predatory to be routine in analyses of African political development. The veil of nation-building was pierced to reveal countries in the hands of what has been described as a 'state bourgeoisie' or 'bureaucratic bourgeoisie' (ibid.: 215), a class whose economic base and power depended on their control of the state. It is in the existence of this class, in Africa and else-where, that the differences in rhetoric about human rights can be located. The scorn poured on the Western version of individualism and civil rights by the class which depends on complete authoritarian control of state power and resources is so easily explicable without resorting to notions of 'culture'.[9]

Some analysts have presented the current phase of African politics, in which the statist economies of Africa have been subjected to the structural adjustment requirements of the World Bank, as one which poses a particular crisis for the development of a rights paradigm in Africa on the grounds that such a paradigm depends on a lively (and culturally based) conception of economic and social rights. It *was* the case that many pre-structural adjustment states paid lip service to such concepts of rights, often elevating them for politically oppressive reasons to a priority over civil and political rights. The interest of the elites of the 'bureau-cratic bourgeoisie' in emphasising so-called 'second generation' collective rights, and thereby sanctifying the increasing sphere of state activity, seems plain. It is probable, however, that few rights of any kind can be achieved without radical changes to the existing polities. Inasmuch as structural adjustment contributes to this (and it may not), it can be said to be contributing to the development of a rights culture. Perhaps the most important lesson to learn is to doubt radically the often repeated mantra that economic and social rights must be achieved before civil and political ones.

A number of features have contributed to the view of the state as culprit in Africa.– growing violence and oppression; the failure of development; the end of the Cold War; the triumph of the market; the emerging dominance of the World Bank. All put the predatory state and the bureaucratic bourgeoisie in the dock. Structural adjustment, as Whitaker says, challenged the class basis, and the patronage politics, of the African ruling class (ibid.: 215). Externally, in place of development strategies the demand was now for a better quality of governance to preserve, protect and enhance the market. This implied a level of stability which could be achieved best through political democracy and fairer and more effective administration. The demand for 'rights' came, therefore, in the case of most of Africa, not as the ideological driving force of an internal political revolu-tion, but as a measure of quality control for the governance of the kind of state approved of by dominant outside economic powers and institutions. (Even in the South African rights revolution this has been a fundamental ingredient.)

The dominant elites of Africa are threatened by this kind of state and by this model of rights, and prefer to mobilise support for their position by invoking versions of collective rights based on state action (and therefore on their own political power). As the foreign-inspired structural adjustment programmes cut into popular areas of patronage it was easier for elites to organise support for their own version of rights against a 'foreign' version which had little basis of internal support to begin with. It was not difficult for the challenged elites to present the different versions of rights in terms of a cultural struggle because in the first place the demand for first-generation civil rights was 'foreign'-supported, and, in the second place, second-generation collective rights, which could be portrayed in culturally collective terms, were compatible with and, indeed, strengthened the elites' control of the state.

The Cold War, in the context of which the African successor states to colonialism were constructed, and in which they developed, explains at the same time the heightened rhetoric about rights, and the lack of concern with securing their effectiveness. States that were economically dependent on, and politically a part of, the West were not subjected to rights audits, the primary requirement of governments being that they maintained themselves in power and did not deliver their populations to any form of communism. Only in the post-Cold War period, when the huge costs of maintaining these structures – in terms of military expenditures, debts and aid – have become evident, has a demand for better government become a Western requirement. One of the languages in which this demand is made is the language of rights, and there is concomitant pressure for the development of constitutional states. Yet while one may (as many Africans do) place the utilisation of rights language in the context of the power which others seek to exercise over African polities, the question of what alternative languages, or methods, there are for achieving a greater measure of justice for the subjects of African states remains. Large numbers of states in the modern world were established on the basis of the right of national self-determination, which was the foundational political right of the international state system over a period from the French Revolution to the end of European colonialism. Yet in the post-colonial and post-communist years, self-determination has become the claim of smaller and smaller fragments, undermining the claims of the existing nation-states. In Africa, while the rhetoric of national self-determination accompanied the end of colonialism, the successor states were not based on cultural or linguistic nations, and provided neither a shared democracy based on citizenship nor a linguistic, cultural or ethnic self-determination. A basic political community, membership of which gave access to rights of all kinds, was thus absent. It may be, therefore, that appeals to rights in Africa should be founded on an appeal to universalism, rather than to local institutions and cultures.

Some further basic thought needs to be given to the nature of Empire's successor states in Africa. The very use of the word 'state' obscures the very real distinctiveness of the political structures which succeeded colonialism, and which were based on its political forms. Colonial state structures were notoriously small, capable of random violence, but not of governing in the comprehensive contemporary sense. The efforts which the successor states undertook to build more comprehensive states, in order to overcome local powers, often through the utilisation of the mass political party, have failed. As Migdal has written,

> Ambitious goals for states – aims of actually penetrating throughout the society, regulating the nitty gritty of social relations, extracting revenues, appropriating resources that determine the nature of economic life, and controlling the most dearly held symbols – have seldom been achieved, certainly not in most of the new or renewed state organisations in the Third World. (Migdal et al. 1994: 14)

What has been witnessed in the past decade is the disintegration and diminishing of the capacity of these efforts. Introducing a rights-based governance into functioning state structures is therefore not the task which faces those who would transform Africa's political institutions. Rebuilding collapsing structures, or, perhaps, building states where none had really been built before, seems to be the first step towards rights-based governance. It is in this context that we should look briefly at the role of the World Bank because its intervention has been so important in the recent history of the remaking of African states. The Bank's claim is that its primary emphasis has been on the 'efficiency' of government as a *sine qua non* of sustainable economic growth (1989: viii). Its use of the term 'governance' came to the fore in its 1989 report *Sub-Saharan Africa: From Crisis to Sustainable Growth*. The intervention of the Bank in Africa was premised on the perception of 'the collapse of public sector capacity' in many countries (ibid.: 8). The claim has been that the efficiency of the management of the country's resources is vital for the promotion of sustainable economic development. While the aim was not the promotion of rights as such (the Bank's remit purportedly specifically excluded the form of political regime), the Bank was, nonetheless, concerned with the political capacity of the state to formulate and carry out policies. While the African Development Bank also laid little emphasis on the political nature of regimes, donors like the United Kingdom, and the OECD specifically linked the World Bank's definition of governance to human rights, accountable government and the rule of law (ibid.: xiv).

Thus while there was a difference between the Bank and the OECD in relation to the overt agenda on rights and politics, the Bank's thrust nonetheless had vital political impact. The World Bank developed its concept to require a move from 'a highly interventionist paradigm of government' towards a smaller state with an accountable bureaucracy which would create the 'enabling environment' for private-sector-led growth (ibid.: xvi, 2). Effectiveness, credibility and accountability of state institutions were linked to privatisation, decentralisation and reduction of government. 'The trend towards *decentralisation of government* ... has become one of the principal ways in which this demand for accountability is being expressed' (ibid.: 13). To those accustomed to thinking about the protection of rights in terms of a state-centred model that emphasises the role of the state as the agency effectively securing rights throughout the territory over which it claims sovereignty, smaller and decentralised government implies a weaker state which would find it harder to 'deliver' rights protection. On the other hand, where the state itself has been the main threat to rights, reduction in its capacity may well be the first necessary step to rights protection.

The Bank did emphasise the need for the strengthening of the legal framework of states in receipt of aid. In line with what has been described above, the starting point was not human rights. In its view, market economies

> require a framework of clear laws and efficient institutions ... Creating wealth through the cumulative commitment of human, technological and capital resources depends on a set of rules securing property rights, governing civil and commercial behaviour, and limiting the power of the state ... this set of rules must be clearly defined and known in advance. In many countries the inappropriateness of laws, uncertainty in their application, weak enforcement, arbitrariness of discretionary power, inefficient court administration, slow procedures, and the subservience of judges toward the executive branch greatly hinder development, discourage and distort trade and investment, raise transaction costs, and foster corruption.

Thus the Bank was involved in projects in Africa to strengthen legal institutions 'relating to property rights and contracts in the context of private sector development loans and credits' (ibid.: 27).

While it was the effect of an inadequate legal system on the business sector that was uppermost, the Bank acknowledged that the 'legal framework also affects the lives of the poor and, as such, has become an important dimension of strategies for poverty alleviation ... Inherent in the concept of the rule of law is the notion of fairness and social justice' (ibid.: 23). But it noted that the wholesale transfer of Western institutions was to be avoided and that the 'effectiveness of legal reforms depends greatly on how reforms take into account the social, religious, customary, and historical factors in a society' (ibid.: 27).

The Bank has always claimed that its Articles of Agreement prohibited it from taking 'political' considerations into account (ibid.: 53). Its position has been, therefore, that 'the focus of the Bank's efforts in the area of human rights is on those rights that are economic and social in nature' (ibid.: 53). There is an irony in the linking of the Bank's aggressively capitalist agenda with the second- and third-generation rights that were once the ideological preserve of communist and socialist rhetoric on rights, especially as it has destroyed the state-based programmes which were supposed to deliver these rights. The Bank's 'contribution to economic and social human rights is embedded in its strategy on poverty reduction ...' (ibid.: 53) Consequently, lending for 'human resource development' had increased (ibid.: 54). My purpose in canvassing the World Bank's interventions into re-structuring the state in Africa in the course of a discussion on human rights and culture is, however, really to suggest that what is to be seen are the limits of claims of rights and cultures. The market, and the legal regime to support the market, are not subject to 'culture' in the Bank's eyes. History and 'culture' are nodded to as afterthoughts only, an icing on the analysis of a culture-free market regime.

In the struggles associated with the collapse of the communist states of Eastern Europe a revived notion of 'civil society' was deployed against the state (Migdal et al. 1994: Ch. 1; see also Ch. 10). Understanding of the deployments and meanings of the concept of culture may well be assisted if it is related to the analyses of civil society. Indeed it is of some interest that 'culture' is rarely invoked in political analyses of Eastern Europe while 'civil society' is rarely deployed in the third world. One fundamental difference relevant to the African context appears to be that culture is often presented as a unified field of practice at a level 'above' and beyond that of individual states, while civil society as a political concept has been related to a plurality of local-level agencies and communities 'below' each state. Situating rights practices in cultures rather than civil society is clearly a very different intellectual and political strategy, and one which is directly suited to the interests of those who favour authoritarian and uniform politics. A 'civil society' as a freely interactive realm outside of the state is a more subversive concept to those who control authoritarian states than that of an overarching culture, especially if the latter can be said to be sustained by a divinely ordained moral and legal order. Yet it has clearly been the case that 'civil society' in much of Africa has been alive and well in both the colonial and post-colonial periods (Chazan in Migdal et al. 1994), and it is to some extent surprising that civil society as the locus of rights has received relatively little attention from African rights scholars.[10]

Constitutions and rights

The inter-cultural debates about human rights have been sharpened by a dual process of legalisation both in the recent growth of international human rights law and in the accompanying globalisation of constitutionalism. International political rhetoric about rights drove the proliferation of international and regional rights instruments, and declarations and covenants assumed the legalised status of treaties. Regional treaties (for example in Europe and the Americas) moved beyond rhetoric to regional courts which could hold signatory states to account for their behaviour towards their citizens. And, as discussed above, states in Africa, in Eastern Europe and elsewhere have, in the post-Cold War era, been expected not only to conform to international rights law, but to re-make their internal political processes to display both democratic and rights-based constitutional government in order to achieve international legitimacy. The irony is that the current strength of rights jurisprudence in the Western world has been contemporaneous with the weakening of the welfare state model. In place of a politics in which rights of substance were supposed to be delivered through the political process, now rights jurisprudence is premised on the possibility of re-situating important allocatory decisions. No longer a part of the constant bargaining and struggle of the political arena, decisions about who is entitled to what are, in the rights-governed future, conceived of as de-politicised and rendered according to a set of legal principles.

Rights and law: land and family

As we near the conclusion of this essay, we need to pursue the rights and culture questions into the realms of law 'beneath' that of constitutions and rights declarations. The areas of family law and land law are most often invoked as falling within the realm of the cultural, and are both often linked also to religion. In industrialised societies this kind of classificatory tie has virtually been broken. Why it should still be made by and for non-Western societies deserves a brief questioning, for it is by no means obvious why some areas of law have retained seemingly secure places in the realm of culture while others relating to basic matters of rights, entitlements, powers and duties (say contract, labour law or torts) have not. Both family law and land law regulate the structural building blocks of rural societies. Land and the reciprocal duties of labour and support provided and provide the necessary means of subsistence for the subordinated peasantries of colonial and post-colonial countries.

It is precisely when the security of access to land, and family support, come under threat and strain that the need to claim them as absolutely fundamental to cultures is strongest. It was, and is, the threatened loss of land which produces the most vigorous claims about its cultural embeddedness and inalienability. And it was, and is, the strains on family organisation produced by the cash economy, migration and urbanisation, and the feared collapse of reciprocal obligations between generations, that make emphasis on the cultural nature of family authority and roles so necessary (Chanock 1998).

Yet enshrining rights in universalised rhetorical form at the highest levels of law can do little to redress the fears and needs of those trapped within these necessary cultural assertions about the customary and traditional forms of family and land law. The complex legal questions about the enduring nature of marriage and disputes over separation, about rights and duties in relation to children, about division of property and access to inheritance, about the duties between generations and kin in regard to mutual support, are not soluble by the invocation of a rights paradigm. Assertions at the level of rights about access to and use of land likewise will not address the questions of population growth, food scarcity, market pressures and responses in relation to rural produce, and the interplay between urbanisation, the desire for security on land, and the market.

Some concluding rhetoric

In concluding I would emphasise three points. The first is in summary of my remarks about culture made above. All that we say about 'culture' comes from a history of imperialism, and from the current dual framework of 'orientalising' and 'occidentalising' in a world of globalised symbolic exchange. If we are to treat 'culture' as a fundamental factor in our analyses of rights, and of government and institutions, we need a very high degree of self-awareness of the history and current circumstances of the deployment of the concept. The rulers of many of the states of Africa and Asia have tried to push rights issues out of the realm of both state and society and into that of 'culture'. And it is into a macro realm of culture, which overarches particular states and societies, that it is placed, rather than in the micro realm of the daily practices of particular and local communities. The macro realm is, clearly, representable as both more legitimate and more resistant to change.

This brings me to the second point. We should ask what narratives are being replaced by the focus on 'culture'. Post-everythingism has not changed everything. In the post-communist world material explanations have dropped suddenly from social analysis. Yet one does not have to be clinging to the wreckage of Marxism, or conspiracy theory, to insist on the need for an adequate account of the material world in which concepts of rights are deployed. The relationships between the rights debates and African poverty, lopsided Asian 'miracles', world trade and international debt must be a part of the analysis of cultural transformation.

Thirdly we should consider carefully the relationship between analyses on the micro and the macro level. Within the framework of the recent African past, the terrible wars in Angola and Mozambique, the long-running oppression of the southern Sudan, the collapse of states in Sierra Leone, Somalia and Liberia, the wars and oppressions in Ethiopia, the implosion of Zaïre, the genocide in Rwanda, all raise the question, at what level do we pitch analysis? Where, in the material, international, institutional and local fields do questions about rights and culture become important?

A focus on rights and culture continues to produce a sacralised discourse which tends to push us beyond the world of known oppressions and empirical political demands and interests. I have attempted to historicise the moment in which this sacralised discourse has come to appear so cogent, and also to suggest that it involves a process of creating 'brands' – both of politics and cultures – in ways similar to the methods of international advertising. I think that there are better ways to approach these questions, and the clearest is through an attention to the detailed articulation of wrongs and needs.

Chapter Two

Contradictory perspectives on rights and justice in the context of land tenure reform in Tanzania

Issa G Shivji

The purpose of this discussion is to explore the notions of justice, rights, democracy and fairness in the particular context of the current debate on land tenure reform in Tanzania. The process was inaugurated by the Report of the Presidential Commission of Enquiry into Land Matters of which I was the chairperson. Subsequent to that, the Ministry of Lands published its National Land Policy, which formed the basis of the draft Land Act prepared by a consultant, Professor Patrick MacAuslan, under contract to the Overseas Development Agency (ODA). Although the draft Act has undergone modifications through its various versions, its thrust has remained the same. The comments in this essay are based on the version of the Act, dated August 1996, which was presented to a conference in Arusha in November of the same year.

The position taken here is that the issue of land tenure reform cannot be separated from the question of democracy facing the country today; that no major law such as a land tenure reform law can work satisfactorily if it does not speak to the major grievances of the large majority of land users – the peasant and pastoral communities; that land tenure reform is not simply a matter of law but an issue of justice. The central question to ask, therefore, is: does the draft Bill embody the notions of justice, rights and fairness held by the Tanzanian people themselves, or is it an expression of attempts to impose typical top-down bureaucratic approaches and notions of 'administrative' justice on the people?

In the first section of the discussion I briefly review Western and colonial notions of justice. Section two goes on to compare the notions of justice and rights which form the basis of the Commission's Report with those that inform the Land Act. This is done by selecting a few issues – such as the vesting of radical title, dispute-settlement machinery and village adjudication – as examples for analysis.

The colonial heritage

'Post-colonial Africa has a triple heritage of law', wrote Ali Mazrui, 'indigenous/ customary law, Islamic law, and the legal and judicial systems which came with Western acculturation' (Mazrui 1989: 252). The last of these is what constitutes largely, if not exclusively, state law, while Islamic law is often subsumed under customary law. Academic discussions of 'competing' notions of justice and fairness in Africa are constructed around this triple heritage, i.e. the notions of justice and fairness embedded in Western law (state law), customary law and Islamic law. To be sure, state law and customary law did not evolve in some kind of separate and independent manner. They were constructed in the course of social struggles and changing material and social relationships. 'Customary law' was used as a resource or ideology of resistance both against the imposed state law and within African communities, as the penetration of a commodity economy created increasing differentiation within societies (Chanock 1991: passim). Nonetheless, the colonial state law ultimately called the shots. It expressed the dominant logic of the state and, therefore, African custom itself became what could be accommodated within the state law. As Chanock observes, 'What was ultimately allowed to develop as "custom" and what was not depended on what the State would accommodate' (ibid.: 80).

While customary law – as well as the notions of justice and rights underlying it – was a contested terrain, it seems to me that some of the more recent literature has tended to exaggerate the contest by ignoring or de-emphasising the dominant contest which was with the colonial state (law). Thus stereotyped notions of customary law portraying communal consensus and idyllic social harmony, while a little exaggerated, may still be closer to the truth. This is certainly so when they are contrasted with the notions of rights and justice which Western law constructed around the fetish of the abstract individual (Fine 1984: Ch. 2). In Western jurisprudence construction of rights is rooted in two sets of theories. One has its origins in the period of the Enlightenment and is based on contractarian constructs. These are indeed the alter ego of the legal contract based strictly on commodity exchange. Here rights are rights of contracting parties (juristic persons) arising from contractual relations (private law) and constructed around, to use Marx's phrase, 'freedom, equality, property and Bentham'. It is this understanding of rights, coupled with Dice's notion of parliamentary supremacy/rule of law, which is strongly present in the rights discourse within the positivist or empiricist tradition that predominates in Britain. In the hands of English courts, the natural law theories of the Enlightenment period were transformed into largely procedural rights under the rubric of principles of natural justice. Substantive rights continued to be constructed around the building block of private contract.

Natural law theories and the notions of natural rights were more influential in the American and French revolutions, which have had greater influence on the discourse on substantive rights and the deepening of the doctrine of the rule of law/separation of powers. The colonial state law was strictly constructed in the crudest positivist tradition as a collection of rules to transmit force. The concepts of 'freedom' and 'equality' were confined to private law contractual relations, while public law did not exist beyond the criminal code, which itself was drained of any rights content as its operation was predominantly an administrative rather than a judicial affair. The colonial executive was the legislature, the administrator and the judge (that is, there was a fusion of diverse powers within the executive). During much of the colonial period, constitutional law and administrative law (both in the realms of justifying and of restraining state and administrative power) were very undeveloped. Thus colonial law was predominantly a self-sufficient body of rules giving widely discretionary powers to officials to control the governed; in other words, it made possible a thinly veiled exercise of state force which was not disguised by ideologies of justice, rights and fairness.[1] Colonial state law is, then, eminently a despotic law. The colonial state, to the extent that it did seek legitimacy, did not do so on the legal terrain, but rather on the cultural, the racial and the religious terrain.

The post-colonial state inherited and further sharpened the authoritarian character of the law. This point need not detain us further as there is considerable literature showing the authoritarian character of African law (for example Ghai 1986, Okoth-Ogendo 1991). The post-colonial state sought legitimacy in various nation-building and developmentalist ideologies (Wamba 1991, Shivji 1986b). In the case of Tanzania, as I have shown elsewhere, the ideology of Ujamaa could be considered hegemonic (Shivji 1995). 'The law' as such was not the terrain for the construction of legitimacy; rather its main function was to control and regulate (Shaidi 1985). The legal order exhibited much more the tyranny of rules than the rule of law. The post-independence state law continued to operate in the positivist tradition, tempered, at best, only by principles of natural justice. In the absence of an enforceable bill of rights, even the constitutional notions of (human) rights (and justice) were, until recently, irrelevant. Equality, justice and rights were constructed on non-legal terrain in the realm of the (statist) ideology of Ujamaa. Within the limitations of its strong statist and top-down character, the ideology of Ujamaa had far greater resonance among the large majority of the popular classes (particularly the peasantry) than any liberal notions of human rights and democracy have had subsequently.

On the other hand, within the official academic and political discourse customary law has had very little presence except as a nuisance which ought to be modernised at the earliest convenience. Thus customary law, if it is considered at all, is viewed primarily as a lived experience subtly expressing itself in the day-to-day perceptions of people and, probably more sharply, in conflictual situations. Academic research on customary law generally, and in particular on customary law as a terrain of alternative perspectives on rights and justice, is scanty. This discussion is therefore not able to draw on any body of secondary material as far as Tanzania is concerned.

What I have tried to do in what follows is to explore people's perspectives on justice and rights as these underlay the complaints and grievances that they presented to the Presidential Commission on Land Matters (Tanzania 1992), which I chaired. Land being their major resource and the site of their construction of culture, custom and conflicts, their actually existing perceptions about land issues should, it is hoped, be able to give us a fair picture of the alternative, and possibly competing, perspectives on rights and justice that inform these perceptions – that is, perspectives which compete with those embedded in state law and policy.

I have gone further to explore how the perspectives of the people on rights and justice, thus expressed, were translated into the policy, institutional and legal recommendations of the Commission for land tenure reform. Since the publication of the Report, the government through its Ministry of Lands has published a National Land Policy (NLP) paper. Basing his work on this paper, a consultant from the United Kingdom, Professor MacAuslan, was hired to draft a comprehensive law to effect reform and regulate land tenure in the country. Having done the draft, the author took the opportunity of the Third Alistair Berkeley Memorial Lecture, which he delivered at the London School of Economics on 30 May 1996 (MacAuslan 1996a), to make jurisprudential observations on his work and provide academic justifications for the policy choices he had made as the consultant draftsperson. The government policy, the draft Land Act and the lecture together supply excellent material to enable one to unravel the dominant state law perspectives on rights and justice. This is what will be done in the following sections, taking a few selected areas dealt with by the Commission's Report and the draft Land Act as examples.

The terrain of contradictory perspectives: land tenure reform

Background to land law

The land tenure regime in mainland Tanzania was established by colonialism in a short piece of legislation called the Land Ordinance, 1923. This is the law which still forms the overall legislative framework for land tenure and 'land rights' in the country. The most important provision is that which declared all lands in the country to be public lands at the disposal of the Governor (now President) and that no occupation of land would be valid without the consent of the Governor (s.4). The effect of this provision was to expropriate control over land from the indigenous or colonised people and vest it in the executive arm of the state. Much of the later development of land law and the tenure system, whether by way of legislation, judicial law-making or administrative practices, was built around this major premise.

The Governor was empowered to grant land by way of a right of occupancy (defined as a right to occupy and use land) for a period of up to 99 years. This came to be called the 'granted right of occupancy' and was the main basis for the alienation of land to foreign companies, settlers and other immigrants, both in the plantation sector and in urban areas. The genius of the colonial judiciary (with the assistance of the Privy Council) regularised the indigenous occupation of land by small peasants and pastoralists by coining the category of the 'deemed right of occupancy', which referred to the occupation of land by indigenous people governed by their respective customary laws. The courts assumed consent on the part of the Governor to the use and occupation of land by indigenous landholders. The legal regime, thus constructed, fitted neatly into a colonial political economy based on a small plantation–mining sector in the hands of for- eign and immigrant capital on the one hand, and a large sector of small peasants producing for the metropolitan market, as well as taking care of reproduction of local labour through food production, on the other.

What is more interesting for the purposes of this discussion is the relationship of what appears on the face of it as the dual land tenure regime (statutory and customary) with the state, and the relationship of the two parts of this regime with each other. The relationship between the state as the grantor and the occu- pier as the grantee of the right of occupancy was contractual. The rights of the parties were determined by a civil relationship based on the fundamental notions of Western legal justice discussed in the previous section. Any breach of the con- tract (that is, any dispute) went to civil courts manned by professional magis- trates and judges, where the highest recourse was to the Privy Council. Where the courts found gaps in statutes they resorted to principles of common law and equity, modifying them according to local circumstances as they were empow- ered to do under the reception clauses. Thus developed the statutory land regime. Like much of colonial jurisprudence, the notions of human rights and justice were strictly jurisprudentially positivist, philosophically empiricist and legally contractual whereas human rights were, according to Bentham, nothing but 'nonsense on stilts'.

The relationship of the customary occupier to the state was statutory (as opposed to contractual). His or her occupation of land, as the courts said, was permissive, almost at the mercy of the state. The relation between the state and the customary occupier was administrative.[2] The predominant function of the state in this regard was one of control, while it operationalised its regulatory function through the customary law. The relationship of customary owners amongst themselves was governed by customary law; their relationship with the state was administrative; and in relation to the statutory or contractual occupier it was that of an inferior. Customary landowners went to traditional courts (chiefs) for redress. Both customary law and customary courts were subordinate to the colonial state executive. Firstly, as the reception clause made clear, criminal customary law was not applicable. Where state force appeared on the surface and, therefore, notions of justice and rights were more openly operative – as in penal law and more generally in public law – the colonial state kept its control intact. Customary law regulated land relations as a matter of personal rather than private or public law. Even here, the higher colonial or civil court had powers to disallow a rule of customary law if it was repugnant to 'justice, morality and good conscience'. While it is true that the so-called customary law was a reconstructed one and embodied the struggles of the people, this was not some process of 'negotiation' or 'dialogue', as post-modernist language would have it.

Secondly, the producer and production on the land, and its management and administration, were under the control of the state, sanctioned by penal law through various regulations and by-laws passed by 'native authorities' on 'advice' (in practice 'directives') of the provincial commissioner.[3] This once again stands in stark contrast to the contractual or civil relationship with the grantee of the statutory right of occupancy, where development conditions, for example, were incorporated as a covenant in the certificate of title. Thus customary law as co-opted by the colonial state was both subordinated to it and disembodied of its own autonomous notions and perspectives of justice.

The post-independence state inherited the land regime outlined above. The most important tenurial reform was the abolition of freehold tenure, which covered less than one per cent of land. The freehold land was converted to leasehold (rights of occupancy) tenure. The other reform was to abolish a semi-feudal system in the West Lake Region known as 'nyarubanja' and to enfranchise the tenants. Both these reforms arose from the philosophy that Nyerere had expounded in the late fifties in response to the colonial government's proposals to individualise, title and register (ITR) land. Nyerere argued:

> If people are given land to use as their property, then they have a right to sell it. It will not be difficult to predict who, in fifty years time, will be the landlords and who the tenants. In a country such as this, where, generally speaking, the Africans are poor and the foreigners are rich, it is quite pos-

sible that, within eighty or hundred years, if the poor African were allowed to sell his land, all land in Tanganyika would belong to wealthy immigrants, and the local people would be tenants. But even if there were no rich foreigners in this country, there would emerge rich and clever Tanganyikans. If we allow land to be sold like a robe, within a short period there would be only a few Africans possessing land in Tanganyika and all others would be tenants. ...

If two groups emerge – a small group of landlords and a large group of tenants – we would be faced with a problem which has created antagonism among peoples and led to bloodshed in many countries of the world. Our forefathers saved themselves from this danger by refusing to distribute land on a freehold basis. (Nyerere 1966: 55–6)

This was integrated in Nyerere's Ujamaa philosophy and policy after independence. In 1962 Nyerere set out the following philosophy on land tenure: 'The TANU Government must go back to the traditional African custom of land holding. That is to say, a member of society will be entitled to a piece of land on condition that he uses it. Unconditional, or 'freehold' ownership of land (which leads to speculation and parasitism) must be abolished' (ibid.: 167). The translation of this philosophy into law did not go further than the abolition of freehold, while the basic principle of 'security of land being dependent on use', which both the colonial state and the post-independence governments argued was a traditional principle, remained intact. What is most significant, though, is that the overarching ownership principle of radical title vested in the state remained, and was further reinforced in that the post-independence state was able to legitimise itself as the representative of the people. Furthermore, as has been shown in many studies, the despotic colonial legal regime (rightless law) continued unabated. The imperial presidency with vast unrestrained powers was the pinnacle of the authoritarian state in Tanzania. As I have argued elsewhere, the state sought political legitimacy not so much on the legal terrain – i.e. in the ideology of legal rights and justice – as in the developmentalist and nation-building ideologies prevalent at the time, and which, in the case of Tanzania, took the form of Ujamaa (see Shivji 1995, 1992).

Ujamaa, drawing its legitimacy from African familyhood, combined in itself notions of human equality (*binadamu wote ni sawa*) and social equity. As the policy of the state-party, these tenets were not embedded in law as such, but were translated into action by state or party or both, often contrary to law. The law, on the other hand, continued to operate on the assumptions of the cold-blooded 'freedom, equality and property' of the contract, which in practice, as has been argued by critics, means inequity for the propertyless and freedom of the property-owner (Fine 1984). Nyerere often made a similar critique of the law on political platforms, castigating law as a pastime of lawyers and courts as football grounds. The result, though, was legally unrestrained actions by the state and its bureaucracy and inevitable abuses of power (see, inter alia, Williams 1982). It is in the most important policy measure of Ujamaa, villagisation, that the tension between rightless law and the Ujamaa variant of social justice revealed itself in the most dramatic fashion around the question of land.

Villagisation involved a massive uprooting of peasant or pastoral communities from their original places of residence and resettlement in villages by coercion, without consultation or consent. Over nine million peasants were resettled in villages. This was done without any authority in law and without regard to the tenure system. The legal justification, never articulated as such, was simple. Land belonged to the state (*'ardhi ni mali ya umma'*); therefore, the state could do with it what it felt necessary in the interest of the people. As it was, under colonial jurisprudence customary landholders hardly had secure land rights in law. The post-colonial state took this situation to its logical conclusion, drawing upon its political legitimacy as expressed in the ideology of Ujamaa. The move backfired with the liberalisation of the 1980s and the abandonment of Ujamaa, as the richer sectors of the former customary owners began to seek redress in law. (The upheaval and the potential for social conflict thus created was one of the reasons which led to the appointment of the Land Commission; see Shivji 1994.)

Nonetheless, the tension (cynically touched upon by Nyerere and which often led him to ignore the law) between concerns of social justice and the law's enormous capacity to co-opt and transform these into, at best, individual procedural rights (natural justice) is one constantly faced by even more radical social reformers and activists.[4] This tension is rendered even more complex because in authoritarian polities, social concerns become statist commands enforced through coercion unrestrained by 'rule of law', which in turn makes the alternative of liberal 'rule of law' as an 'unqualified good' something to struggle for, attractive as an end in itself.[5]

This is precisely the kind of dilemma which was faced by the land commissioners. On the one hand, there were statist structures and practices abusing their powers against the large majority of, particularly, rural and peri-urban landholders. On the other hand, the alternative offered by the liberal Western law and human rights, in its construct of (individual) rights and procedural notions of equality, freedom and property, fell woefully short of the demands and interests of the village communities and socially disadvantaged groups and classes. This came out clearly in the evidence presented to the Commission. The discussion that follows centres on how, in its recommendations, the Commission sought to resolve this dilemma and the tension between alternative perspectives of justice and rights that it conveys. This is compared and contrasted with the justice and rights perspectives underlying the proposed Land Act drafted by MacAuslan.

Rights and justice perspectives in the Land Commission and Land Act

The Land Commission: background

The Land Commission visited all districts of mainland Tanzania except two, and held some 277 meetings in 145 villages and 132 urban centres which were attended by over 83 000 people. Over 3000 people submitted their complaints and opinions (Tanzania 1992: 2–3). On the whole, therefore, the Commission was able to gather a fairly wide and representative sample of people's grievances against the existing system, their suggestions on reform and their underlying perspectives on rights and justice, which were often made explicit in narration of anecdotes and concrete examples. The chairperson of the Commission, in a preface to the published Report, claims that 'the *Wananchi* were not only the foundation of inspiration to the Commissioners but the ultimate source of major ideas presented in the Report. What we did was to systematise, articulate and present in a coherent manner what we had gathered from the people in the language of their daily experience and practical wisdom' (ibid.: xii). Maybe this was a little exaggerated in so far as the institutional and legal structures recommended by the Commission are concerned. But there is no doubt that the basic underlying principles were crystallised from the perceptions and practices of the people as recorded in evidence.

Ownership and control of land

The single most important source of complaints and grievances was identified by the Commission as lack of participation and consultation of the people in the decision-making and administrative processes relating to land. '*Hatukushirikishwa* ['we were not consulted, we didn't participate'] was the constant cry. ... The demand for participation was not made in any general fashion but with respect to specific issues of administration of land' (ibid.: 94). Non-participation was thus both the source of complaints and abuses as well as a democratic demand which informed the major recommendations of the Commission on reforming the land tenure structure, institutions and law. A democratic demand to be consulted and participate as of right on matters involving the major resource around which the living conditions, culture and customs of the majority of producers are constructed is a social-democratic demand; the core of this conception of justice may be summed up, albeit inadequately, in the notion of social justice. I have argued elsewhere that the right to participate and be consulted by the people might be captured within a reconceptualised notion of the right of peoples to self-determination (see Shivji 1997). This is not the place to go into the details of these arguments. Suffice it to say that the perception of the villagers in Tanzania, as described here, comes very close to the theoretical arguments made by Archie Mafeje in his intervention on the debate on democracy (1995: 5–28). Critiquing African scholars who posited values and state structures of liberal democracy as an alternative to the statist one-party authoritarianism in Africa, Mafeje argued that they simply missed the boat both in their historical understanding of the democracy discourse as well as in their understanding of the real living conditions of the oppressed classes (the large majority) in Africa. Arguing that, while genuine democracy might be difficult to achieve, it was not difficult to define in the present conditions in Africa, Mafeje submitted that ordinary people 'only fight when their livelihood is threatened'. In other words, 'they fight in order to guarantee the necessary conditions for their social reproduction' (ibid.: 26).

> Regarding the present conditions in Africa, this can refer only to two things: First, the extent to which the people's will enters decisions which affect their life chances; and, second, the extent to which their means of livelihood are guaranteed. In political terms the first demand does not suggest capture of 'state power' by the people (workers and peasants) but it does imply ascendancy to state power by a national democratic alliance in which the popular classes hold the balance of power. The second demand implies equitable (not equal) distribution of resources. Neither liberal democracy, imposed 'multi-partyism' nor 'market forces' can guarantee these two conditions. It transpires, therefore, that the issue is neither liberal nor 'compradorial' democracy but social democracy.

The Commission translated the message embedded in the battle-cry 'hatuku-shirikishwa' to mean the demand to democratise the land tenure system in which the villagers and the peri-urban and slum dwellers would participate, either directly or through elected representatives, in making major decisions relating to land. The Commission had to face head-on the existing statist land tenure system in which the radical title to land, and thus ultimate control, is vested in the executive arm of the state, which, in practice, meant the Ministry of Lands and its subordinate bureaucracy. On the other hand, there was the market model market (ITR – individualisation, titling and registration) advocated by the dominant IFIs (International Financial Institutions), Western donors and their foreign consultants. Neither of these models, as was very clear from the grievances and demands of the large majority, accommodates the essentially social-democratic perspectives of the peasant, pastoralist and so-called squatter communities. The Commission had to recommend policy, institutional and legal reforms in land administration which simultaneously responded to the demands of the people and also provided a feasible alternative for organising the land tenure system. The main features of the Commission's recommendations may be summarised as follows.

Firstly, the monopoly of radical title vested in the head of the state and executive, the President, should be broken and the radical title should be diversified together with the administration of land. It was recommended that all lands in Tanzania should be divided into national and village lands, and that national lands be vested in a Board of Land Commissioners under the National Lands Commission (NLC), which would hold them in trust for the people of Tanzania.

The village lands would be vested in respective village assemblies which would be composed of all adult members of the village. Village assemblies would be the ultimate owners, controllers and administrators of village lands. Village assemblies would have a fixed quota of women in attendance.

Secondly, the NLC would be responsible and accountable to the parliament (National Assembly), the most representative body at the national level. While the President would nominate the land commissioners and the chief executive of the NLC, they would have to be confirmed by the National Assembly, through its land committee, in public hearings.

Thirdly, at the primary level, all the processes concerned with land delivery – surveying, planning, allocation and registration, and dispositions on national lands – would be done in public through the participation, and under the supervision, of elected ward and district committees. At the same time, no land would be considered ready and available for allocation unless certified by the circuit land courts. Thus judicial intervention would not simply happen *ex post facto* to provide redress but as an anticipatory measure to prevent abuse.

The Report goes into great detail on the administrative, institutional and legal dimensions of the NLC. The central recommendation, however, is undoubtedly the divestiture of the radical title and de-linking of land from the executive and vesting of village land in the village assemblies. This recommendation is the most fundamental one and runs through all the more detailed recommendations of the Commission. Admittedly, this would have some significant impact on the organisation of the state structure.

Both fundamental recommendations of the Commission – the divesting of radical title and the vesting of village lands in village assemblies – were unequivocally rejected by the government and find no place in the draft Land Act. The National Land Policy paper described the existing land tenure system, whose main feature is the monopoly of radical title, as 'fundamentally sound' (Tanzania

1995: para 9). The earlier draft of the policy paper was even more forthright, if rather unsophisticated, in its defence of the monopoly of radical title.

> The existing legislation on land and a long experience and practice of more than 30 years after independence, vesting all land in Tanzania in its President and granting of Rights of Occupancy to the rest of the population has shown that the present land tenure systems [*sic*] is a sound land tenure for Tanzania. The President is holding the said land in trust for all the citizens of Tanzania and land being a basic element of the State, the Head of State (the President) can easily acquire a piece of land for use for the benefit of the people. ... To detach the Head of State from land would be a radical departure from the present land tenure system. Such a change is just like making him and his government beggars for land for implementation of government development policies and projects. (Tanzania 1993: para 8)

It is curious how the feudal notion of the identity between sovereignty and property in the absolute monarch reappears in the bureaucratic or authoritarian state. In other words, just as a king without land could not be conceived of in feudal Europe, so an 'imperial' president without control over land is considered a beggar in a republican Tanzania! MacAuslan skirts around this issue in his lecture, which otherwise tries to justify various policy decisions he says he had to make in drafting the Land Act. At best, he offers a lame defence by asserting in his commentary on the draft that 'no government is willing or should be expected to give up that power', having in the first place, incorrectly in my opinion, identified the vesting of radical title in the President with the powers of eminent domain (i.e. of acquiring land for 'national and public purposes') (MacAuslan 1996c: 14).[6] The historical fact is that the vesting of proprietary title in land in the state was eminently a colonial creation and was recognised as such by some contemporary commentators. (See, for instance, the discussion in Meek 1946.) This principle, which both the policy paper and MacAuslan's commentary call 'fundamental' and which means, in the words of the commentary, that 'all powers over public land stem from the president', is what is reflected in the draft Bill. As a matter of fact, the Commissioner for Lands, as a chief delegatee, so to speak, of presidential power, has far more powers (spelt out more explicitly and in great detail in the draft Land Act) generally, and particularly over village lands, than the existing political and administrative practices allow. Be that as it may, what is clear is that the notions of social justice, equity and rights of the villagers as evidenced in the narratives before the Commission – and which the Commission translated as a demand for the democratisation of land tenure – cannot be squared with the detailed legal structure of the draft Land Act, which takes the top-down statist approach (i.e. vesting of land in the President) as its primary building block.

Whereas the Commission explicitly recommended the de-linking of land ownership and administration from the executive, the draft Act actually re-inforces this link at both the national and village levels. In this process the central actor is the Commissioner for Lands in the Ministry of Lands. At the village level, the role of the village assembly is almost totally sidelined while the village council (an elected body of twenty-five persons) is the main manager and administrator of village lands. The powers of the village council are regulated with detailed provisions. The ultimate supervisor of these powers is the Commissioner. Under certain circumstances the Commissioner can even take over the administration of village land from the elected village council (cl. 59(7)(c)(ii)).[7] In short, rather than the village council (village government) being accountable and responsible to the village assembly (village parliament), the village council is accountable and responsible to the appointed officer of the central government, the Commissioner for Lands. To cite one, not atypical, provision, the village assembly may complain to the Commissioner where it feels that the village council is not exercising its functions properly. It is the Commissioner who has the legal power to issue directives to the council and, if need be, take over the management of the village land from the village council. At the village level, democracy is stood on its head by inverting the position of the organ of direct participation, the village assembly, and the elected body, the village council, on the one hand, and by making the elected body, the village council, accountable to an appointed official, the Commissioner, on the other.

The detailed management, administration and adjudication structure set out by the draft Act is reminiscent of the disastrous 1972 decentralisation process which was put in place by an American consultancy and management firm, McKinsey (Coulson 1982: 254 ff). It decentralised central state bureaucracy to regional and district level and abolished elected local governments. It was such a disaster that the whole structure had to be reversed six years later, doing irreparable damage to the government machinery (see Mushi 1978, for an excellent study).[8] The administrative procedures, with their endless forms and constant seeking of directives and advice from the Commissioner in terms of the draft Act, amount to nothing less than the setting up of 'mini-ministries of land' at village levels which, even by conservative estimates, would require at least three to five paid officers – a clerk, a typist, an accountant, a cashier, a messenger and a professional scribe to help villagers fill in prescribed forms! – in the more than 8000 villages of the country, a total of 40 000 people in a country which is declaring thousands of its more senior civil servants redundant! It would require constant communication with the Commissioner in Dar es Salaam (within set time limits) in a country where many villages are not easily accessible and mail takes weeks to arrive, if it ever does.

In this regard, the draft Act is centrally based on giving powers to state officials, albeit subject to very detailed provisions, while leaving administration in the hands of village-level elected officials constrained by equally detailed provisions but with little power or discretion. The draft Act betrays its penchant for positivist legal justice (or more correctly, 'administrative justice' in the colonial sense to be discussed below) and a distrust in ordinary people and their elected representatives, particularly at the local level. In this it shares the values, assumptions and biases of modernisation and developmentalist scholars, and those of the 'law and development' school, whether liberal or authoritarian.

Machinery for dispute settlement and administration of land rights and justice

One of the major findings of the Commission was that the machinery for resolving land disputes had virtually broken down (see Tanzania 1992: Ch. 10). Firstly, there was overlapping jurisdiction between various bodies, including organs and members of the executive and the party, that were involved in resolving disputes. Secondly, disputes lasted long periods without final, conclusive and certain determination. Thirdly, organs of justice were remote and inaccessible both physically and socially. Fourthly, the people showed great dissatisfaction with the decisions of judicial organs. They did not find them just and fair. The following narrative before the Commission is typical:

> My rights are customary. CDA [Capital Development Authority, a parastatal] found me on the land. They allocated the land to the person I regard as an invader. He took me to a court. He produced a certificate as proof of his ownership of the plot. The court ruled against me and awarded the invader my land. I did not accept the injustice and I stayed on the land. The invader took me to court again, this time on a charge of criminal trespass. I was arrested and locked up till I was released on bail. I went to the appellate district court. I lost the appeal. I became very angry to no avail. The invader has since mortgaged my land and secured a bank loan. So I sit on my land as part of the mortgage. (ibid.: 204)

A fifth way in which this machinery manifested its weaknesses was that government organs, including courts, were accused of nepotism, corruption and bias. In short, the people accused the so-called machinery of justice of inefficiency, illegitimacy and injustice. Clearly the state organs of dispute settlement had lost credibility. People demanded organs that would be impartial, nearby, accessible and accountable to them. In this case, the Commission found that the traditional bodies such as elders (*wazee*) still commanded respect and legitimacy as mediators and arbitrators of disputes. In recommending the machinery of dispute settlement, the Commission was guided explicitly by the principle that people should have faith in the legitimacy of the dispute settlement machinery; that the organs of justice should be accessible, approachable and comprehensible; and that they should be open, transparent and institutionally impartial and independent. In a word, the Commission was both conscious of, and deliberately tried to move away from, the Western positivist bias towards professional dispensers of justice (who were seen to be 'qualified, competent, efficient, objective').[9]

Combining these principles, the Commission recommended the *baraza la wazee* (elders' council) as the basic village organ with original jurisdiction in all land matters, both civil and criminal. Five *wazee* would be elected by the village assembly for a period of three years but could be recalled by the assembly before the end of the term under certain circumstances. The *baraza* would be independent of the assembly and the village council in its operations and determine all disputes (including those against the council) in open meetings in accordance with customary law, principles of natural justice and the community sense of fairness and reasonableness. The *baraza* would also double up as a body to register customary titles (in a village land registry), again in open meetings. Thus the process of registration was seen as a judicial process.

Appeals from the *baraza* would go to Circuit Land Courts, which would be presided over by a professional magistrate assisted by a panel of *wazee*. The *wazee* would give their own reasoned opinion as to what they considered to be the just and fair outcome of the case before them. While the magistrate would not be bound by the opinion of the *wazee*, he or she would be required to give reasons for either agreeing or disagreeing with them. Further appeals would go to the Land Division of the High Court and there, too, a judge would sit with a panel of *wazee*, who would have a similar role. The Commission explained the role of the *wazee* as follows:

> We see their role as somewhere between the existing system of assessors and the jury system in some common law jurisdictions. It will be noticed that our conception of their role is closer to a jury system than our assessors system. This will allow a fuller participation of the community in the process of adjudication over land. But, even more significant, our expectation is that by exposing the professional personnel (such as magistrates) to the values of justice and fairness of the community, the system will help to develop a more legitimate corpus of law and procedure having roots in the values of the community. (Tanzania 1992: 202)

In this deliberate manner the Commission tried to bring into the open the competing perspectives on justice between Western-trained legal professionals representing legal justice and community elders expressing alternative views. Furthermore, the Commission wanted to move away from the racially structured dualism of colonial times under which jurisdiction depended on the law applicable to registered or unregistered land, the assumption being that registered land was governed by statutory Western law while unregistered land was governed by customary law ('native law and custom') and the 'elders' only sat as some kind of advisers (or appeared as expert witnesses) in matters involving customary law. In the words of the report,

> These dichotomies are in fact a remnant from the colonial past. In the colonial society the dual judicial structure significantly corresponded to the racial structure. English/statutory law had connotations of superiority over customary law just as registered land was considered to enjoy greater and legally protected security of tenure compared to unregistered land. Soon after independence the court structure was integrated, thus doing away with the overt racial division. But other dichotomies based on the laws applicable or whether the land was registered or unregistered, with all its implications, were maintained, and in some cases resurrected, in post-independence statutes. (ibid.: 199)

The draft Land Act adopts the terminology of the Commission's Report in setting up the dispute settlement machinery, while disembodying it of all its principles and perspectives on justice, community participation and development of a more legitimate Tanzanian common law.

In the draft Act the *baraza* is composed of persons nominated by the village council, approved by the village assembly and confirmed by the judge of the Circuit Land Court (cl. 218). Its jurisdiction is only in civil matters confined to the value of 500 000 shillings where both parties agree to submit it to the *baraza*, and 200 000 shillings provided the matter in dispute is governed by customary law (cl. 219). The Circuit Land Court is headed by a professional judge who sits with two advisers selected (cl. 217(9)) from a panel of Regional Customary Law Advisers appointed by the Judicial Service Commission 'to assist the circuit land court judges in that region in determining cases involving an issue of customary land law' (cl. 217(7)).

The Circuit Land Court has jurisdiction in all land cases governed by received law (cl. 217(8)) of value not less than 25 million shillings and cases involving customary law of value more than 200 000 shillings as well as appellate and supervisory jurisdiction over *mabaraza*.

The Land Court (which is at the level of the High Court) is similarly composed of a judge who sits with customary law advisers in matters involving customary law (cl. 215). It has original and appellate jurisdiction throughout mainland Tanzania.

The post-Arusha Bill has made further modifications to the machinery for settlement of land disputes. The *mabaraza* have disappeared both in name and in substance. At the village level, instead, there are only panels of mediation whose jurisdiction is voluntary. Parties to a dispute need not submit to the panel's jurisdiction at all, and even if they do so, the panel's decisions are not binding. It is the primary courts which have original jurisdiction in matters governed by customary law or unregistered land within specified pecuniary value. The Circuit Land Courts are called District Land Courts in the modified draft. For all intents and purposes, the proposed machinery for settling land disputes will be what it is at present, and the changes are more tangential than substantial. In other words, the mass of evidence collected by the Commission that the existing machinery (primary and district courts) is neither efficient nor commands the trust of the people has made no impact.

The draft Land Act, in its provisions concerning dispute settlement machinery, reveals in an even more open fashion the biases of Western positivism and its notions of legal justice. To add insult to injury, it resurrects the colonial divisions between received law (not defined but presumably covering statutory law, common law and principles of equity) and customary law. Professional legal justice is dispensed by professionally trained judges applying received law, in which they are supposed to be well versed. When matters involve the laws and customs of the community, the judges are not supposed to be well versed and, therefore, sit with 'advisers' who are members of the community. However, the 'advice', i.e. the notions of justice and fairness of the community, is subject to the sense of justice of the professional judge who has the final decision-making power. Even the decision as to who may act as advisers cannot be left to the community concerned, but is left to the judgment of the professionally constituted Judicial Service Commission. Where small landholders (those with property not worth more than 200 000 shillings) are concerned, and their matter is governed by customary law, it can be decided by the village-based *baraza*; presumably the quality of justice does not matter where the pecuniary value of the subject matter is small and the disputants are small village fry! (These comments apply with even greater force to the post-Arusha draft.)

Clearly, this conception of top-down professional legal justice based on 'received imperial notions' of justice, fairness and reasonableness clashes directly with the conception of rights and justice of the large majority of the Tanzanian land users on which the Commission based its recommended structure. Several biases mentioned here, and the general bias against the popular classes, come out in MacAuslan's justificatory lecture.

Citing precisely the jurisdiction and procedures of the *mabaraza* as recommended by the Commission discussed above, MacAuslan observes,

> these far-reaching proposals involve changes in the law but the clear message of the Presidential Commission was that the new law should be similar to that which it will replace in terms of drafting style; a few broad strokes of the legal pen giving vast powers to totally *unqualified people* and relying on their innate common-sense and sense of justice to get things done; just like Operation Vijiji in fact. In the light of the evidence uncovered by the Presidential Commission of the abuse of power and the chaos that accompanied that exercise, the word 'naiveté' comes to mind to describe this approach. This might be unfair; a better analysis is that the approach adopted by the Commission is a classic example of the operation of 'path dependency'. (MacAuslan 1996a: 12–13) [emphasis added]

Then the author goes on to cite an obscure passage from an equally obscure writer on what is called 'path dependency',[10] whose relevance is difficult to understand, and continues,

> Applied to land and the use of law to alter land relations in Tanzania, this tells us that while the policy proposals of the Presidential Commission were indeed far-reaching, the approach to the use of law to implement them was driven, to some extent by long-standing Tanzanian legal traditions which stretch back to colonial times [sic!]. The real revolutionaries therefore might turn out to be not those who propose radical policies but those who, through the NLP [National Land Policy], propose a radical legal methodology for implementing policies; namely a detailed and inevitably lengthy new land code in which legal rules and checks and balances replace reliance on administrative and political action based on goodwill and common-sense; on the evidence, in short supply where land relations are concerned. (ibid.: 13)

It is interesting, to use a mild term, that the author likens the Commission's approach to law to that of the colonial tradition. It is true that the drafting style of the Land Ordinance itself was 'a few broad strokes of the legal pen giving vast powers'. The major difference, though, is that these powers were given not to an 'unqualified' mass of 'natives', 'relying on their innate common-sense and sense of justice to get things done', but to the highly qualified servants of Her or His

Majesty such as the Governor and the Commissioner, backed by state force trans-mitted through law. It is also true that 'Operation Vijiji' was not operationalised through law and there were lots of abuses. But these abuses were not committed by 'unqualified people' 'relying on their innate common-sense'; rather they were committed by very qualified 'public managers' sent closer to districts and villages in the process of decentralisation recommended by another consultant, McKinsey & Co., Inc. (see Coulson 1982: 252 ff). 'The "operations" were organ-ised by the Regional Commissioners (or Regional Party Secretaries) assisted by the experienced civil servants who had been sent to the regions and districts in 1972 "decentralisation" ...' (ibid.: 252). As to whether the Commission or the draftsperson of the Land Act has been 'driven ... by longstanding ... legal tradi-tions which stretch back to colonial times', the analysis on the resurrection of colonial dichotomies in the Land Act discussed above should offer some help in resolving the issue.

The approach of the Commission to law, legal rules and 'checks and balances' was deliberate and clear. Given the longstanding Tanzanian tradition, stretching back to colonial times, of giving wide discretionary powers to government organs and officials (including the then Governor, now the President, of whom the com-mentary states graphically, 'all powers over public land stem from the President'!), without consultation of and reference to the people's innate sense of justice and fairness, the Commission provided for more rules to control the offi-cials at the top while giving larger discretion to elected organs (for example, *baraza la wazee* and people operating at the bottom). The purpose and aim of this provision, too, was clear. The Commission wanted to create an enabling legal framework which would let ordinary people's sense of justice, rights, fairness and reasonableness jostle for hegemony with the 'imperial/colonial/positivist' notions embedded in received law – 'common law, principles of equity' – relied on by the professional dispensers of justice. As a matter of fact, the Commission recom-mended that the definition of customary law should be broadened to include local customs as recognised by a Tanzanian community or neighbourhood, as well as 'native law and custom' (Tanzania 1992: 188). The Commission further recommended that the traditional subjection of customary law to the standards of justice, good sense and morality of 'white' colonial judges (the 'repugnancy clause' in the reception statutes) should be turned on its head by means of a pro-vision that the received common law and principles of equity should not be 'repugnant to Basic Principles of National Land Policy and principles of justice, fairness and equity held in common by Tanzanian communities' (ibid.: 192–3). What is more, the *wazee*, selected from the *mabaraza ya wazee* elected by village assemblies, should sit with the magistrate in the Circuit Land Court and the judge in the High Court in all cases, not as advisers on customary law (as if to this day customary law is some foreign law to our judges), but to impart the community's sense of justice and fairness and force the professional judge to take full account of this perspective.

As for checks and balances, the Commission took a further radical step by applying the venerated liberal constitutional principles of separation of powers and independence of the judiciary at the village level and not simply confining it to the state level. Thus the *baraza la wazee* was supposed to be an impartial, independent judicial organ used not only in resolving disputes but also in adjudication and registration processes. The draft Land Act, on the other hand, harks back to the colonial tradition of the hated 'administrative justice' and fusion of power. (Recall that the district commissioner was also the magistrate!) Thus the executive organ at the village level, the village council, has powers to impose penalties, including fines, for breaches of conditions (see cl. 87) although under certain circumstances such a remedy has to be approved by another executive organ of the central state, the Commissioner (cl. 87(2)). Yet the independent judicial organ, *baraza la wazee*, has no criminal jurisdiction whatsoever, thus resurrecting the colonial rationale that the administration of penal or public law could not be entrusted to the 'irresponsible' 'traditional authorities'. (The post-Arusha Bill has modified slightly the provisions on breaches. The point of principle, however, remains. The Commissioner has powers to impose penal sanctions under customary law for breaches.)

Adjudication and issuing of certificates of customary occupancy

Adjudication of land rights and the processes of registration and issuing of certificates of customary occupancy (*hati ya mila ya ardhi*), in terms of the Commission's recommendations, is pre-eminently a judicial process involving basic land rights, which should be conducted in an open meeting where any member of the village community has a *locus standi* to object to or support and supplement an application. The Commission reviewed the process of started adjudication in Kenya in the 1950s to individualise, title and register land held under customary law. There have now been a number of studies to show that the virtues attributed to ITR are simply not borne out in practice. In fact, the process works against the interests of the disadvantaged in society.

What is more, the whole process is extremely expensive. It means adjudicating and processing millions of titles. Therefore the Commission recommended that there should be no ITR, and opted instead for a more feasible village-based process of issuing *hati ya mila ya ardhi*, which would be done by the village body, the *baraza la wazee*, and records kept at the village level.

According to the draft Land Act, adjudication and issuing of certificates of customary occupancy is primarily an elaborate bureaucratic process under the administration of the executive organ, the village council ('advised' by the village adjudication adviser, a professional person, appointed by the Commissioner), which is accountable to another executive organ, the Commissioner for Lands. Under certain circumstances, the Commissioner may even set aside village adjudication and impose central adjudication. In many ways, the draft has 'smuggled' in the process of ITR through the back door. For all intents and purposes the processing of the certificate of customary occupancy is not fundamentally different from processing a granted right of occupancy. In practical terms, such a massive project of titling villagers' lands is virtually impossible. In fact, the whole process is fraught with enormous practical problems and injustices are likely to result, as has happened in Kenya. In short, the whole sub-part 3 of Part VII of the Act requires very careful consideration.

The idea of land associations (sub-part 4) to enable groups to register is reminiscent of Kenya's Land (Group Representatives) Act of 1968 and Tanzania's Range Development and Management Act (RDMA) (see MacAuslan 1996b: 54–5). The latter, which arose from a UNSAID proposal, was a failure. The Kenyan Act has come under critical review; some studies have shown that in pastoral areas the Group Representatives Act has in fact meant control by richer members, who have in turn sold off lands to 'outsiders', to the detriment of the majority of indigenous people. It is surprising that the draft Act should resurrect land associations in spite of this experience and the experience of the RDMA.

Leaving aside the practical and virtually unanswerable argument that the whole section on village adjudication is simply impossible to operate in Tanzanian villages, the point is that the conception behind the whole process of adjudication is that it is an administrative and management issue which cannot be entrusted (a) to an elected village organ without ultimate control and (b) certainly not to the village judicial organ, *baraza la wazee*. This brings me to the final issue of the Act's approach to law and, therefore, to the perspective on rights and justice implicit in it.

Reform through law

The Commission's view was encapsulated in a threefold approach. Firstly, the main contours and parameters of the land tenure system should be included in the constitution so as to entrench it in public law and give it visibility. Secondly, there should be a Basic Framework law spelling out the broad principles and rules of land tenure. Here the approach taken was to propose that there be more rules and procedures requiring transparency and accountability on the part of government officials and organs towards elected committees and other representative bodies, to control the exercise of government power. At the same time, there should be greater flexibility, discretion and space for a community's sense of fairness to permeate the lower level of the legal process, as well as mechanisms for facilitating the exposure of the professional functionaries to the locally evolved wisdom of the people as expressed in their customary practices. Thirdly, there should be continued application of customary law to village tenure, albeit in a manner fundamentally modified by the broad democratic principles embodied in the constitution and the Basic Land Law. *Wazee*, for example, are traditionally not elected; in terms of the Report's proposal they have to be elected democratically by the community. Other modifications were proposed specifically to address the gender bias against women in customary law, such as having the names of both spouses on the certificate of tenure, and giving no consent to disposition without consultation and agreement of the other spouse and children.

In effect, the Commission neither wholly rejected nor accepted uncritically the law or legal methods to effect a radical reform of the tenurial system, but was concerned to reform the statist, top-down institutional structures so as to create space for the forces, conceptions and perspectives of the people to assert their interests. At the same time, the Commission rejected the thoughtless parroting of dominant positivist and liberal market approaches to commoditisation of the land in a blanket fashion so as to create an enabling environment for the so-called foreign investor.[11] The Commission clearly identified the path of development (national agrarian), the site of accumulation (village), and the agency (the rich or middle peasantry), and located tenurial reform in this larger context of political economy.

The approach to law of the Land Act is a far cry from the kind of considerations briefly touched upon above. As I have noted, the argument is simply for more law, and that on its own is considered 'revolutionary'. The basic question of what more law will effect, and whose interests it will serve, is of course not asked. Whether there are issues of social justice and equity involved, and how these could be addressed, does not even seem to be a serious concern in Professor MacAuslan's Memorial Lecture, in which he justifies his role as the consultant engaged to draft the Land Act. Normally, it would be unfair to hold an ordinary consultant accountable at this level, because he cannot do anything more than to interpret the policy brief given to him by those who employ his services. If that had been MacAuslan's sole defence, one would probably be wasting time arguing. But the Memorial Lecture specifically sets out to argue that the consultant was very much involved in making policy choices, and not simply engaged in a technical exercise of drafting law. It is therefore only proper that he should be held academically accountable for the particular choices made by him and which he sets out to defend and justify.

Conclusion

In the final paragraphs of his lecture, MacAuslan turns to the role of an academic lawyer and argues that the major challenge of scholarship in respect of land reform in Africa is

> to rise above the merely descriptive and analytical approach to writing about land law and adopt a more policy-orientated and innovative approach which offers new models and creative ideas as solutions to practical problems of land management and, if the opportunity presents itself, become involved in the challenging business of turning these ideas and models into legislative drafts; let no one suggest that that is not a scholarly endeavour. Creative not just critical scholarship is needed. (1996a: 38)

Undoubtedly, no one would argue that academics ought not to be involved in policy debates and offer creative ideas. There is nothing new or original in that, at least not for the academic lawyers of the University of Dar es Salaam. The question, as always, is: 'creative' for whom, and destructive to whom? That is not a new question either, for it has been part of the debate by, and about, intellectuals in Africa, although with the onslaught of a new type of scholarship called 'consultancy' we may fast be losing the capacity to raise questions of intellectual commitment. The debate on the different perspectives on justice and rights embedded in MacAuslan's draft Land Act and the Commission's Report (both being the products of academics) raises a question of a different order from that posed by MacAuslan himself. What kind of perspective on justice, fairness and equity are we advancing when we, as academic lawyers, become involved in law and policy reform? First and foremost, do we accept that (a) there are contradictory perspectives on justice and fairness and that these are neither historically nor socially universal, and (b) that by making certain policy choices (even within the narrower confines of paid consultancies) we may be involved in creating methods and structures which advance certain perspectives while suppressing or delegitimising others?

MacAuslan concludes with an interesting thought which raises a host of questions for many of us who in one way or another are involved in the current 'market-driven' reforms at various levels in Africa. 'In sum, while land law reform might, just, still be the preserve of the lawyer, the products of that reform – the new laws – are the property of the nation and the nation must be stimulated wholeheartedly to embrace those laws. Only in this way can law be made to work to restructure land relations in Africa' (1996a: 39). Why is land law reform 'still the preserve of the lawyer'? Is this because the 'unqualified' people who form the large majority of the nation may find it too technical and, therefore, beyond their reach? Or is it because the legal reforms we are proposing or involved in have not had the people's input? If the challenge of legal scholarship is to be creative and innovative, is it not possible to innovate or reform in a fashion which will translate the interests, perspectives and notions of justice and fairness of the large majority into law – or at least attempt to do so? If that is not attempted, then can we and do we have the right to expect such a law to become the property of the nation?

These are precisely the questions that have been raised in this discussion. The perspectives of justice, rights and fairness embedded in the law reform recommended in the Commission's Report are contradictory to those underlying the draft Land Act. The two perspectives are not only contradictory but locked in struggle. In this contestation one of the perspectives is undoubtedly proving its capacity to become dominant by the logic of force (as exerted by the state). But whether it can also become the property of the nation – i.e. hegemonic – is a different issue. The draft Land Act and the National Land Policy which forms its basis have not been publicly debated. Rather, they were discussed in closed workshops attended by invited people by virtue of their various qualifications, whether political or professional. A call for a public debate of the policy (see Shivji 1996) has been simply ignored while the sponsors of the consultant, and other sources, have been very keen to see to it that the draft Land Act is steamrolled through parliament as soon as possible.

Have the people really accepted the policy underlying the draft Act? In a few workshops held by HAKIARDHI (an NGO), whose main aim is to popularise and facilitate a debate on the Commission' Report, people have largely endorsed the Commission's recommendations, being wary of what is suggested in the draft Land Act (see *Rai*, February 1997 issues). Clearly, then, such a law, if passed, has little chance of becoming the nation's property.

A national consensual legal ideology, it seems to me, cannot be constructed other than through contestation between the existing Western–statist–liberal concepts of justice and rights and the social democratic conceptions and perceptions ('*hatukushirikishwa*', the right of people to life and self-determination) of the large majority, the popular classes.

Finally, it must be emphasised that if the law is to have legitimacy and therefore be workable, it must be debated by the public. What is crucial to its success is how far the people have participated in developing its major basis.

Chapter Three

Were the critics right about rights?
Reassessing the American debate about rights in the
post-reform era

Kimberle Crenshaw

The project of mobilising human rights to facilitate cultural transformation in Africa, and the historical project of mobilising civil rights discourses to effect cultural transformation in the United States of America (USA), have both been situated between competing perspectives on the overall utility of rights. In broad terms, both projects are situated between, on the one hand, the liberal celebration of rights as the principal discourse promoting human liberation and, on the other, trenchant critiques that characterise rights as discourses of domination and legitimisation. In more specific terms, human rights are fêted by some as the embodiment of universal values in history's march toward transcultural enlightenment. They are simultaneously assailed by others within a discourse of cultural authenticity as conduits of Western power under the shadow of colonialism. Similarly, civil rights within the American context have been hailed as singularly capable of transcending racism and parochialism in the linear march toward civil equality; simultaneously, civil rights have been 'trashed' as a co-opting and demobilising discourse of legitimisation.[1]

While debates about the value and utility of civil and human rights are not entirely parallel, there are apparent correspondences between the two that suggest that comparative analyses may be productive. With regard to the specific project of mobilising human rights as a discourse of cultural transformation in Africa, the most immediate point of comparison is not simply the parallel polarities of the rights debate. Instead, it is in the common effort to stake out an 'in between' position that simultaneously acknowledges and resists elements of both the celebration and the critique of rights. Those who seek to develop human rights practice reflective of African cultural contexts stand in a position similar to USA race theorists who sought to defend the liberal aspirations of civil rights while critically interrogating the very terms of the discourse. Both the attempt to create a culturally grounded human rights discourse and a critical defence of civil rights discourse seem contradictory to those who stake out polar positions on rights.

Yet this positioning within the interstices of competing discourses on rights is of a piece with other projects, including, for example, the project of mounting a race-conscious anti-essentialist critique of law ('Critical Race Theory') and constructing an anti-patriarchal discourse on racism and post-colonialism ('Black feminism') (Crenshaw et al. 1995, Crenshaw 1989). In all these efforts, critics seek to synthesise a politics that fuses and resists key elements of the competing discourses in which they are engaged. Given the perils and possibilities of such a reconstructive project, the central information I hope to bring forward for comparative purposes is an account of a particular historical negotiation between what appear to some to be contradictory and mutually exclusive positions on rights.

Beyond the parallels in the positionality of this project and those within the USA are other correspondences that may render a historical overview of civil rights in the (African) American context relevant. Contemporary human rights and civil rights discourses share a common philosophical genealogy. Yet more importantly, they are institutionally related. As Makau wa Mutua points out, international non-governmental organisations (NGOs) 'more than any other [group] have set the agenda and scope of the worldwide human rights movement'. Among the most influential of these are the INGOs that are the 'ideological offspring' of domestic NGOs in the United States. The leadership, priorities and values of such INGOs reflect 'circumstances of their origin'. To the extent that their vision of human rights has been grounded in the context, content, and mechanisms of the domestic deployment of civil rights, an analysis of how rights have performed there would further contribute to ongoing efforts to interrogate dominant conceptions of rights and to develop divergent interpretations that are appropriate here.

The human rights discourse has reproduced a triumphant vision of the role of rights in securing transformative social change. It would seem, however, that the exporting of a celebratory vision of rights should be coupled with critical perspectives as well. Yet the somewhat congratulatory promotion of rights victories predictably leaves its critics and failures at home. As Mahmood Mamdani queries, 'Is it then surprising that what has been handed to us in the colonial world as the "Western tradition" is none other than the standpoint of the dominant classes in the West? And yet, for that very reason, it is this that we need to examine critically and analytically'. In amplifying Mamdani's insistence on such a critical engagement, this essay seeks to provide additional material for such an interrogation.

Civil rights: a post-mortem

The reading of civil rights reflected herein is positioned as a post-reform analysis. By that I mean to indicate that the era in which civil rights produced meaningful reformist victories has come to a decided close. No longer do advocates look to courts or Congress to provide enforceable mechanisms of reform under the banner of civil rights. Indeed, civil rights practice today consists largely of rearguard actions meant to protect hardwon concessions against pressures of retrenchment. As such, the moribund civil rights discourse is offered up and taken apart to identify dynamics surrounding its demise. Of course, the objective is not to identify definitive explanations; any number of factors contributed both to the successes and the failures of civil rights discourses. More importantly, factors that contribute to the current state of civil rights in the USA need not play a similar role in the development of human rights discourse in Africa. They may, however, present researchable questions or points of debate. The same is true with regard to the productive aspects of civil rights discourses.

The central observation arising out of a critical review of civil rights confirms that rights discourses can both facilitate transformative processes and insulate and legitimise power. Needless to say, this theme is not new: it is sounded by critics of human rights, law and development and other liberal-based reformist projects (Trubek & Galanter 1974). Again, Mamdani argues, 'Reform may be the cutting edge of a political programme designed to undermine on-going initiatives; whereas, in other contexts where the initiative lies with the forces of repression, reform could just as easily be the opening chapter of a developing struggle against those forces' (Mamdani 1990). Civil rights deployment in the USA illustrates how these processes occur simultaneously; indeed, the processes of transformation and legitimisation are mutually reinforcing products of the same dynamic.

The critique of rights

The crystallisation of this theme reflects a particular historical moment in the stalled progress of civil rights reforms. During the late 1960s and early 1970s, the high expectations of civil rights advocates, scholars and activists were reinforced by numerous forces. 'Faith flooded in from the outside, at just the moment when liberal lawyers found that their rights arguments had an almost magical effect on the liberal judges with whom they shared the agenda of adjudicatory empowerment' (Kennedy 1997). Not only courts but legislators as well seemed sympathetic to a vision of civil rights attuned to the task of chipping away not only at the formal dimensions of white supremacy, but also at its historically produced structures. Civil rights doctrine embraced for a short time what Alan Freeman labelled a 'victims perspective', a view of equality that sought to intervene in the material, lived-in realities of racial disempowerment. Courts analysed and frequently rejected legislative, executive and even private policies that, due to the historical patterns of subordination, effectively discriminated against African Americans as a group. Discrimination was thus interpreted in terms reflecting what the 'victim' experienced rather than what the 'perpetrator' intended.

Remedies surpassed the sometimes narrow formulation that remedies should extend only as far as necessary to rectify a specific violation of a right. Courts seemed to embrace the notion that the disparate conditions of African Americans were inherently suspect; institutions and actors that contributed to those conditions, whether or not they alone caused the disparities, were often made to share the burden of remediation. Such burdens sometimes included limitations of traditional rights, such as rights to property (white businesses could not exclude patrons simply because of their race), contract (whites generally could not refuse to contract with an African American solely on account of race), unfettered movement of capital (redlining and other banking practices were precluded), and minimally regulated discretion in employment (employers could not use tests and other devices that disproportionately disadvantaged African Americans without clearly rational reasons). These expansive interpretations were backed up by belief that the Constitution authorised these interpretations along with philosophical theory that supported reform on behalf of suppressed groups (Kennedy 1997).

During the heady period of civil rights expansion, the gales of the coming retrenchment were felt only as nippy breezes amidst otherwise balmy winds bringing change. Yet Supreme Court decisions slowly began to reflect the fact that there were competing interpretations of civil rights that might, if fully developed, impede the progress that so many had come to expect. Most troubling were early decisions that seemed to represent a shift from sympathetic 'victim'-based perspectives to a less productive 'perpetrator' perspective. Indeed, courts gradually cut back on the scope of reform, drawing increasingly narrow bounds within which civil rights advocates were required to prove a civil rights violation. No longer did conditions such as massive housing segregation, wholesale exclusion from a range of professions and institutions, marked disparities within the criminal process, ongoing income disparities and high rates of poverty and disease constitute presumptive conditions slated for remediation. Nor were these considered background conditions that social and institutional actors were required to accommodate in pursuing their desired course of action. Instead, in order to invoke civil rights as a basis for intervention, one had to prove that a challenged condition was directly caused by a specific act of a singularly prejudiced (almost irrationally so) actor bent on a course of action, not in spite of but because of the race of those harmed. This narrowing scope of civil rights created a corresponding concept of innocence for all those who were not 'perpetrators'. It also created an agnosticism toward the historical or contemporaneous causes of white dominance and black marginalisation across American social relations.[2]

As civil rights advocates sought to reset the course of civil rights, critics within the progressive wings of the legal intelligentsia began to voice criticisms of the very project of civil rights, criticisms that framed these reversals as an inherent feature of liberal rights discourse (Tushnet 1984, Gabel 1984, Freeman 1978). While many advocates who had come to rely on civil rights discourses were troubled by these analyses, they were perplexed and sometimes angered by the prescriptive message behind the critique – an abandonment of rights discourse altogether. Many received this message as condescending and naive. Specifically, critics within the legal studies movements ('Crits') made several claims against rights discourse. Rights discourse, they argued, was indeterminate and incapable of providing predictable and concrete outcomes. Values and arguments capable of mandating progressive reform existed alongside values and arguments that could very well insulate the status quo. Rights were, in addition, abstracting and demobilising, deflecting the attention of the masses from the more important question of 'needs' and activists from the all-important assessment of whether rights-based activities were politically effective actions. False consciousness figured into the critique as Crits argued that legal consciousness constituted ideological barriers to the ability to imagine fundamentally different social relations. For African Americans, the belief that there existed an imaginary civil society of 'rights bearers' was a sheer fantasy, a flight from reality that effectively induced the oppressed to consent to their oppression. Rather than infusing rights with normative resuscitation, Crits urged that they be smashed in order to open up possibilities of more transformative reform.

While the traditional civil rights advocates tended to reject the Crits' analysis almost in its entirety, some advocates, activists and intellectuals found themselves 'in between' the apoplectic defenders of rights and the irreverent Crits. For those in between, the Crits had articulated what appeared to be a deeply troubling dynamic of civil rights. As the pace of reform had slowed, justifications for limitations were increasingly articulated in the very language of rights that advocates had in a certain sense 'owned'. And the problem was not simply that courts refused to intervene to alter the distributive mechanisms in society that continued to produce racially predictable outcomes. More troubling was that the Supreme Court was beginning to intervene to stop efforts by public institutions and others to voluntarily adopt race-conscious policies to alter societal outcomes, and that the Court was doing so by invoking the civil rights of whites.

Thus, the Supreme Court struck down the policy of reserving set seats in medical school, a strategy designed to increase the number of minority doctors, under the argument that since it denied whites the right to compete for *all* of the seats 'solely' because of their race, it violated their civil rights. In doing so, the Court rejected arguments that the policies were justified on the basis of societal discrimination (too amorphous and timeless in its reach into the past) or legitimate as a method of increasing the quality of health care in under-served minority communities (no indication that minorities will necessarily meet this need). Here and elsewhere, the Court deployed the individual rights paradigm to reject any semblance of group equity under civil rights.[3]

While the courts increasingly rejected institutional approaches that equated substantive equality with some notion of parity between historically defined groups, society at large took on the language of civil rights and the corresponding language of equal opportunity. Yet the performance of equal opportunity was often formal and purportedly procedural: one could be an equal opportunity employer with an all-white workforce. To the extent that civil rights leaders and other opinion-makers had articulated black demands almost entirely within the ambiguous language of equal rights, they were left without a morally or politically convincing discourse to contest the re-deployment of civil rights as a status quo discourse. Thus, the Crits were largely on target in their critiques of civil rights as indeterminate and potentially co-opting.

Yet there remained certain sensibilities about rights that were mischaracterised or under-analysed by the critique of rights. Central among them were the false-consciousness critique and the prescriptive advocacy of abandonment. Neither seemed to engage the historical realities of the African American struggle against both public and private racial power. The effort to respond to the Crits' under-valuation of rights also produced a response to the liberal exaggeration of rights. To the Crits, civil rights transformed insurgents into victims of false consciousness while to liberals, civil rights inevitably pulled hapless blacks into its grand historical sweep toward civil equality. Both visions denied black agency in fashioning a remarkable movement out of the strategic deployment of the ideological materials at hand.

A centrepiece of the modern civil rights movement was the strategic deployment of rights rhetoric to produce a crisis in the otherwise accommodating relationship between local and national governmental power. Civil rights activists hoped to provoke a crisis that would force the national government to act to enforce existing civil rights, as well as to guarantee new rights. For example, sit-in demonstrators and freedom riders publicly defied local authority in hopes that the predictable response of segregationist state and local governments would prompt federal intervention. As predicted, Southern states unleashed both public and private forces of repression. The national government, however, was loath to intervene. Southern whites sought to defend their 'way of life' as culturally sanctioned by the course of Southern history; proprietors of restaurants and businesses argued that equality violated their civil rights (particularly against involuntary servitude) and politicians angrily denounced any hints of governmental intervention as a violation of the sovereign rights to 'handle' the race problems in the way they saw fit.

In an apparent nod to the cultural relativists and the militant sectionalists in the segregationist South, the moderate President Eisenhower seemed to intimate that it might be foolhardy to intervene in such circumstances. 'Law', he opined, 'could not change what lay in the hearts of men.' Despite massive Southern resistance and tepid support at the national level, civil rights protesters and advocates maintained an unrelenting campaign to force open contradictions at certain pressure points. The key pressure point was, of course, the increasingly tense relationship between federal and state authority: eventually, with threats to the safety of school children, freedom riders and even Martin Luther King, federal authority was forced to send federal troops into the South to enforce 'civil rights'.

This effective manipulation of rights discourse appears to be in a different universe than the narrative about civil rights told by the Crits and liberals. The interventions in the South were neither the product of a blind faith in the incantations of rights demands nor the consequence of an automatic extension of rights protections. Yet there remains from the critical perspective a critique of false consciousness at the level of mass mobilisation and, from the liberals, a critique of pure cynicism at the level of civil rights leadership. To this it might simply be said that the very articulation of a civil right by a community which had for generations been denied such rights was transformative, and therefore real at an existential level, notwithstanding the success or failure of the right to bring about material change. The same might be said of advocates: one need not believe in the inevitability nor even the exclusivity of a particular interpretation to escape the liberals' charges of cynicism. Certainly, it is possible to maintain a healthy belief in unrecognised rights as the way things ought to be, and act as if it reflects the way things are. Even the committed indeterminist will acknowledge that sometimes 'as if' performances are later 'certified' by courts and other state actors as legitimate.

While these responses do provide alternative interpretations of the function of rights, particularly at the level of implementation, there remains nonetheless the thorny problem of both the discursive ambiguity of rights discourse and, from the vantage point of the post-reform critic, the problem of legitimisation. Thus, the Crits' case for abandonment remains unaddressed.

To be sure, the case for abandonment seems stronger in light of the trajectory of rights discourse following the initial skirmishes between Crits and their counter-critics. Tendencies and contested doctrinal development have now fully matured into a fully articulated colour-blind jurisprudence. In post-reform civil rights discourse, historical dynamics of white supremacy are wedded to contemporary debates over race-conscious remedial strategies in a manner that proclaims their essential similarity. As Justice Thomas, the justice who replaced civil rights visionary Thurgood Marshall, framed the issue, affirmative action and other race-conscious governmental policies share a 'political and moral equivalence' with white supremacist policies of the past. Thus, whites who can compete for only ninety per cent of all governmental subcontracting are harmed in the same way as blacks and other minorities who were wholly barred from competing for any such opportunities. Or, as one justice pointed out, under this formalistic rubric, the internment of Japanese Americans in World War Two is the moral equivalent of programmes seeking to acknowledge the special contributions Japanese American soldiers made in pursuit of American interests.

These two policies can be made the same in the abstract by framing a particular social theory – that of colour-blindness – as the sole constitutional principle mediating the articulation of equality. The right is now articulated as a right against colour-conscious decision-making regardless of the purpose or intent of the policy. Liberal civil rights advocates continue to wage a rearguard action against these interpretations, arguing alternatively that such an interpretation of the prevailing equality doctrine is historically inaccurate and constitutes an illegitimate imposition of an undemocratic judicial preference over the democratically produced policy decision. A critical race theory approach would, in addition, draw parallels between the emergence of colour-blindness as a constitutional principle and the courts' historical wedding of *laissez-faire* free market economic theories to the liberty rights protected by the Constitution. Liberty of contract jurisprudence is now wholly repudiated in mainstream legal discourse. Constitutional law in the period that bears the name 'liberty of contract' is now regarded as having insulated capital from meaningful reform of its excesses and legitimised super-exploitation of American workers under the rhetoric that designated the exploitative terms of their employment contracts as the product of 'free choice' rather than 'economic coercion'.

Colour-blindness is now poised, under civil rights law, essentially to legitimise the continuing relations of power between communities of colour and whites under a logic of racial *laissez-faire*-ism. A key feature in this newly emerging paradigm is the re-deployment of culture as a marker for race. While civil rights reforms are framed as having fully rejected race-based assumptions that African Americans are inherently inferior, racial *laissez-faire*-ism permits differential values assigned to individuals and communities on the basis of advanced or disabling culture. Thus, continuity in the material status of African Americans is consistent with a fully functioning regime of civil rights because expectations of cultural equity have never been guaranteed.

The discomfort with this newly minted racial *laissez-faire*-ism under the rubric of civil rights is not only grounded in the recognition among many that for all intents and purposes African Americans have 'lost' the struggle over the expansive or narrow definition of civil rights. It is more broadly grounded in the sense that the recent losses are re-deployments of mediating principles and interpretative strategies that prevailed during the nineteenth century's installation of the doctrine of separate but equal. For example, in *Plessy* v. *Ferguson*, the court interpreted segregation to be consistent with equality by sharply distinguishing the civil and the social realm, and applying the narrowly framed principle of symmetry to define the scope of civil equality. Thus, segregation was consistent with civil rights because African Americans and whites were treated symmetrically: African Americans could not sit in cars reserved for whites and whites could not sit in cars reserved for African Americans. Of course, the subordinating dimension of segregation was found not in the absence of formal symmetry but in the presence of contextual asymmetry: segregation was unequal because of its message of racial inferiority and the attendant inequalities in spaces marked off as 'black' and white.

Nonetheless, the court relegated the asymmetry of segregation to the unprotected field of the social, where the message 'received' by blacks was simply deemed a matter of 'choice'. The court in *Plessy* opined that if blacks were ever to be treated as social equals, they would have to convince whites of their social worth, not through legal discourses, but within the 'social' marketplace. Implicitly, interpreting civil rights to require social equality would constitute an illegitimate redistribution of social capital to those who had not 'earned' it, in much the same way that a century later, courts would claim that redistributive policies constituted an unconstitutional end-run around the economic and cultural marketplace.

Plessy serves as a sober reminder that the most important dimension of civil rights is the mediating principle that determines how any given right will be articulated in context. This is where indeterminacy manifests itself: there is no way to guarantee or articulate in advance how a right will be applied in context. If this problem stood alone, it might be said simply that rights constituted an arena of chance in which there is a minimal entry fee and a potentially large payoff. Yet the relationship is a bit more vexed than this image reveals. In *Plessy*, and in modern jurisprudence, the existence of formal rights provides some degree of legitimacy for claims that the location of various groups is the product of their aggregate 'value' as determined by an unencumbered 'market', and further concessions are thus unjustified and unnecessary.

At this point one might take seriously the Crits' prescription of abandonment and take up the search for an alternative discourse promoting social transformation. There is, however, a nagging sense that the critique reflects a vision of transformation somewhat ironically situated in bourgeois visions of social transformation. The prescription seems to follow along an assumption that, having identified vulnerabilities in the strategy for reform, there must exist another way 'out'. For elites, perhaps, there are no structures in which there are no exits; the task is simply to find them. Yet, perhaps the experiences of resistance struggles suggest that one of the features of relative disempowerment may be that whatever strategy one chooses is fraught with counterproductive dynamics that may well swallow up or significantly alter the articulated goals of struggle. Indeed, in terms of the language of rights, the relationship between winning and losing may be perversely linked.

In the context of the civil rights movement, the articulation and subsequent enforcement of rights was not automatic but was the product of efforts to politicise a contradiction between dominant ideology and certain material realities. Sometimes such contradictions force elites to close the gap or to render the conditions somehow consistent with dominant ideologies. Thus, barriers might be lifted, or formal rights might be granted, yet the scope of the reform is probably limited by the dynamic that gave rise to the contradiction-closing gesture in the first place. Circumstances may be adjusted only to the extent necessary to close the contradiction. As argued earlier, 'although it is the need to maintain legitimacy that presents powerless groups with the opportunity to wrest concessions from the dominant order, it is the very accomplishment of legitimacy that forecloses greater possibilities' (Crenshaw 1988).

It may thus be the case that insurgent movements find themselves attempting to negotiate between rocks and hard places. If it is true that rights discourses can sometimes be simultaneously transformative and legitimising, then strategies must be found to minimise the risks inherent in engaging in potentially co-optive discourses.[4]

Conclusion

I have attempted to summarise various dynamics found in USA civil rights discourses that may be germane to efforts to mobilise rights discourses in pursuit of cultural transformation in Africa. Although I have positioned the role of the engaged critic as partially parallel to the culturally invested human rights proponent, I am aware that the latter project diverges in numerous ways from the historical narrative set forth above. Here I wish only to make a few comparative comments on some of the features of the cultural transformation project. Herein specifically are concluding comments about sovereignty, culture and gender.

To a large extent, the 'success' of the rights paradigm in the USA was facilitated by the particular relationship between federal courts and the dual sovereignty of the American federal system. Federal courts were simply crucial in articulating a vision of equality that was transformative; ironically it was their non-democratic constitution that placed them outside the reach of angry majorities. The counter-majoritarian dimension of American courts presents a special problem in the African context, as protection of minority rights at the expense of popular democratic process creates a significantly different dynamic. Yet placing the weight of human rights articulation and enforcement within designated interventionist institutions may be crucial in creating interventions not for the powerful minority, but for the powerless groups, whether they be majorities or minorities. Such institutions need not be seen solely as constituting top-down interventions but instead as providing institutional structures ready and able to back up the demands of disempowered groups in the negotiations with other groups and entities. Indeed, at the level of strategy in the USA, rights 'worked' in that their assertion by protesters and the repressive response of state and local governments forced a coercive intervention by a more powerful entity on their behalf. Rights 'failed' to the extent that there was no higher court of appeal in the wake of Supreme Court retrenchment.

The importance of an external coercive force in the American rights context is further suggested by the relative failure of race reform protests as they moved north. Courts as well as politicians were less receptive to interventionist demands as the movement travelled from the region in which racism was seen as the product of a backward culture to the Northern region where racism, equally virulent, was managed as a policy of informal power rather than state policy. Yet the distinction between white supremacy as a product of state policy and white supremacy as the aggregate effect of informal state and private power was materially inconsequential. Indeed, there was, by and large, greater segregation in living, employment and educational patterns in the North. Yet protesters in the North could not rely on any outside force to compel a recasting of the distinctively Northern style of racism as an *ipso facto* violation of civil rights.

While coercion constitutes the unpleasant underbelly of the domestic civil rights narrative that is exported through human rights organisations, coercive dynamics seem to run counter to the image of reform envisioned under the Cultural Transformation Project. This in turn raises the question of at what level and in which arenas the current Project is located. Where and how are human rights articulated and enforced? As between a formal state ideology and an insurgent discourse within popular struggles, the Project seems to be clearly located in the latter. Yet, in seeking transformation that is continuous with culturally legitimate discourses and avoids the critique of compromised sovereignty, its location and level of articulation are difficult to identify.

Along these lines, I refer back to the deployment of culture by the South in defence of white supremacy. The defence was ultimately unsuccessful because the weight of public opinion outside the South and among blacks within the South rejected it. Of course, to the extent that culture is defined in terms of common practices, meanings, and customs, it would be hard to reject the notion that there was a cultural dimension to white supremacy. Yet activists and the liberal intelligentsia understood the 'culture' of the South to reflect the reification of dynamics of power in law and in custom. To the extent that there was always resistance within that culture, the South could lay no claim that its side of the 'debate' should be privileged over the historical pockets of resistance internal to it. Moreover, critics rejected the idea that Southern 'culture' could lay claim to an unmediated historical practice. To the extent that national power, which resided in the North, permitted Southern practices to proceed through a regulatory posture that included both action and inaction, Southern culture could be seen as the product of an interaction between Northern regulatory schemes (self-determination while policing the 'excesses') and white Southern power. Thus, the claim that enforcement of civil rights constituted an invasion of the South by the North denied the extent to which the North was 'already there'. Through its acts and omissions, the Northern political elite shared some responsibility for the practices that survived. Another feature of this analysis is the manner in which Northern permissiveness in the South served Northern interests, particularly among the political bosses of the Democratic Party. There was thus no hermetically sealed Southern culture in the South, and no 'clean hands' in the North.

Turning back to the project at hand, the spectre of the West imposing its values in the shadow of colonialism is of course a far more troubling concern than the complaint by white Southerners that the federal enforcement of civil rights constituted a reoccupation of the South by a 'foreign' presence. Yet what exactly is to be made of the difference? Is it a matter of degree or is there a fundamental distinction between claims of empowered elites here and those elsewhere that reformist policies flying under the banner of rights constitute an affront to culture and sovereignty?

Another interesting divergence between rights and culture, as deployed in the Cultural Transformation Project and in the American civil rights context, is suggested by the aspiration to facilitate transformative dynamics in a manner distinct from the highly contested politics of brinkmanship detailed above. Central to the narrative of transformation in the USA was the manufacturing of crisis and the creative exploitation of contradictions. On the one hand, it seems that the American experience bespeaks a sharp break with popular traditions and practices; it would be difficult to imagine any way to achieve some sort of consensus that the presence of African Americans beside whites at lunch counters and at the front of the bus was nothing other than a repudiation of practices that whites saw as constituting their heritage. On the other hand, if transformation is facilitated through the resolution of erupting contradictions, then the consequent synthesis is both continuous and discontinuous with the pre-existing social order. So, while it might be claimed that highly politicised and deeply contested dynamics of rights production commanded from below render the hope of consensus-based transformations unlikely, it is also true that any resolution of such demands will reflect some interaction of existing cultural material with new or immanent interpretations.

Of relevance to culture as well as politics is the quite provocative dynamic out of which discourses of anti-imperialism reify and in some ways insulate conditions of disempowerment among subgroups in African society: women, peasants, religious minorities and the like. The spectre of an invasive external power and the discourse of resistance to it is mobilised in internal contests to rationalise the rejection of demands for reform. A very similar dynamic is apparent in the political debates internal to the African American community. There, patriarchal practices and the marginalisation of the struggle against sexism are reinforced and amplified through the privileging of a specifically gendered (male) narrative of racism. Paralleling the manner in which the history of colonialism is invoked to muffle the demands from below, the deployment of various tropes that position African American men as racism's primary target in the USA provides the consensual basis for a distinctive patriarchal rhetoric and practice. Shored up by appeals to a common goal of fighting racism, black women's simultaneous interest in contesting sexism is marginalised within antiracist politics.

Black feminists have attempted to augment the historical memory of group oppression with narratives of black women's oppression. They have sought to reveal how contemporary understandings of racism are narrowly gendered, and fail to fully incorporate black women's gendered experiences of racial oppression (Crenshaw 1993). This project is critical in contemporary politics, given the centrality of black women as a symbolic target in domestic efforts to cut social welfare. However, recent events such as the Million Man March and the rallying of African Americans around figures such as O. J. Simpson, Mike Tyson, Clarence Thomas and others suggest how sexism and patriarchy are deeply entrenched in black resistance politics. The effort to mount a human rights-based discourse that resists the almost effortless stigmatisation of gender equity as alien and distracting constitutes yet another common 'position' from which African American feminists and African human rights could engage cross-culturally.

The foregoing analysis has not engaged the remaining feature of the Cultural

Transformation Project, namely religion. Formally, this may be the area in which there is the greatest divergence between civil rights deployment in the USA and human rights articulations in Africa. Religion within the American context is rather firmly entrenched in the private sphere. Indeed, its emergence in politics has deeply troubled traditional civil rights advocates and has been allied with forces of retrenchment discussed above. Yet, there are two features of religion and its intersection with civil rights that bear mention. Firstly, the defence of legal rights by critical race theorists and others was premised on a pragmatic recognition that rights consciousness was the only real contender to contest the dominance of white race consciousness in the pre-civil rights era. Similarly, the rejection of the Crits' call to seek out alternative discourses was based on a belief that no other discourse had emerged to fill the consensual and coercive role of legal discourse. This localised analysis of the unavailability of alternative discourses – including religion – is quite obviously likely to diverge in other contexts. Thus religion, in conjunction with human rights, might well provide an amplifying discourse that was unavailable in the USA. One hastens to note, however, that some of the dynamics observed throughout rights discourse might still obtain. Indeterminacy at the level of articulation and implementation is likely to be replicated in religious discourse, along with the presence of interpretations that co-exist with and run counter to certain human rights aspirations. The instrumentalities and mechanisms of consensus-building and coercion remain significant as well.

Finally, any analysis of the civil rights movement would be remiss in failing to acknowledge the role that the organised black church played in mobilising and sustaining mass insurgency. Martin Luther King's brilliant invocation of higher moral principles no doubt provided the insulation against corrosive forces of doubt and official repression that could have crippled the movement. Yet for the most part, the churches' discourse of morality and the law's discourse of rights did not formally intersect. On occasions where they were at odds – for example, in Dr King's invocation of a higher moral authority in defending his refusal to obey a federal court injunction against a specific protest – religious discourse was summarily subordinated to the law. Perhaps one can conceive of a different relationship between religion and law – one that does not presume the superiority of one over the other. Yet the simultaneous deployment of two discourses each asserting a particular claim of allegiance may also set the stage for the eruption of a 'crisis' between two authorities similar to that which produced the moderate 'success' that civil rights has come to represent.

Chapter Four

State, community and the debate on the uniform civil code in India

Nivedita Menon

The tradition–modernity opposition

The debate on the Uniform Civil Code (UCC) in India is, at one level, the enacting of a spectacle all postcolonial societies are familiar with – a dramatic confrontation between 'modernity' and 'tradition'.[1] It is in this sense that the form this debate has taken in India would find itself confronting a myriad of reflections in the African context – strange yet familiar. The difference in the histories of our colonial experience shapes our contexts in specific ways, but there are familiar echoes, fleeting glimpses of recognition. The UCC debate is a story about the struggle for women's rights to inheritance, to equal status within marriage and upon divorce; in short, for equality within the family. But the UCC debate is also about the rights of religious communities to their ways of life, and the protection of such rights as an integral part of India's democracy. In one telling of the story the force of modernity is the hero, liberating women from the chains of tradition, and in another telling, tradition is the quiet and dignified defence against the alienating, dislocating thrust of modernity.

Mahmood Mamdani (1996: 3) characterises Africa's present predicament as presenting two clear tendencies, the modernist and the communitarian. The former derives inspiration from the East European uprisings of the 1980s, focuses on civil society (as yet embryonic and marginal) as the space of democratisation, and champions the language of rights. The latter calls for a 'return to the source' – that is, to African traditions – urges the placing of communities at the centre of the democratic process, and counterposes culture to rights.

Thus, despite the specificity of the two contexts, the shared experience of encountering modernity mediated by colonialism has shaped the modern self both here and there in mutually recognisable ways. But the time has also come, it is clear, to problematise both poles of this all too familiar binary opposition of tradition–modernity so that we can mark the uniqueness of this historical moment as 'our' moment of modernity. First, we need to contest the way in which critiques of modernity are understood to emanate only from within tradition, and critiques of tradition from within modernity. The political task is precisely to deconstruct this binary opposition in order to demarcate (and recognise) a third site from where we can scan our landscape. From this site it becomes possible to see that modernity and tradition are not always two clearly distinguishable moments. What is called tradition, especially in postcolonial societies, is unavoidably located within modernity, and irretrievably constituted by modernist discourses. Neither pole of the opposition remains hermetically sealed from the other. There is a vast body of scholarship in our societies which demonstrates that 'custom' and 'religious practice' have been decisively fashioned by colonial administrative fiat. Yet these categories continue to be engaged both intellectually and in political practice, as if they were primordial.

Furthermore, we recognise from our vantage point in the 'third site' that critiques of each do not only come from the other. Modernity, that is, comes under attack not only from tradition but from opposing tendencies within itself, and similarly tradition is challenged not only by the language of rights and modernity but is internally contested in its own terms. These internal contestations tend to be obscured by the ritual ways in which these categories are invoked.

A politics of radical democratisation would have to recognise the specific oppressiveness of both modernity and tradition. For feminists especially, this is a crucial step to take because in postcolonial societies tradition seems to offer a refuge from the alienation and commodification set in motion by modernity. One kind of feminist critique of the new ways in which forces of modernisation oppress women can be cast in terms which valorise the premodern space of tradition. But of course, at the same time, feminist critique has to be aware of the oppression which is institutionalised by tradition, and against which the values and institutions of modernity offer weapons of critique. Thus we continue in many senses to be trapped inside the swing of this particular pendulum, unable to make a critique of modernity and tradition simultaneously.

Consider the instance cited by Thandabantu Nhlapo[2] in order to attack the pretensions to universality of the modernist discourse of rights. He referred to the case of a beauty queen criticised by and debarred from functions of the Society for the Prevention of Cruelty to Animals because she declared at a press conference that she would celebrate her victory the traditional way, by slaughtering an animal. Nhlapo used this incident to outline a defence of the rights of communities to their traditional ways of life against the overwhelming homogenising drive of modernity. As I see it, however, this is a good example of what I have termed the prison of the pendulum – the inability to escape the tradition–modernity opposition. In other words, what is also at stake in this episode, but rendered invisible in Nhlapo's telling of it, is modernity not just as the force eroding the traditional rights of communities to their ways of life, but modernity as the force which introduces a particular kind of objectification of the female body. Nhlapo remains unaware of the irony of defending the 'traditional' forms of celebration of the community in this specific context: what the woman in question is celebrating of course, from a feminist perspective, exemplifies the commodification and alienation of self, particularly of the female body, which is typical of modernity.

The point I wish to make is that modernity runs counter to an emancipatory ethic in several ways, and tradition is only one of the lenses through which this may be made visible. In fact, modernity itself offers the values which can form one basis of attacking it. Indeed, autonomy, equality and freedom, which Nhlapo has invoked in the instance cited to defend the right of the beauty queen to celebrate her victory in the way she chooses, are themselves archetypically modern values. Our political practice needs to work on the delineation of the 'third space' from which a critique of both tradition and modernity can be made.

The UCC debate

First, it would be helpful to outline the contours of the issue. The debate over the UCC in India is produced by the tension between two notions of rights in the Fundamental Rights section (Chapter III) of the Constitution. The bearer of rights is both the individual citizen and the collective; the former is the subject of Articles 14–24 which ensure the individual's rights to equality and freedom, and the latter of Articles 25–30, which protect religious freedom and the educational and cultural rights of minorities. It is from the latter that religious communities derive the right to be governed by their own personal laws.[3] Since these personal laws cover matters of marriage, inheritance and guardianship of children, and since all personal laws discriminate against women, the tension in Part Three of the Constitution is at one level a contradiction between the rights of women as individual citizens and those of religious communities as collective units of this democracy.

The demand for a Uniform Civil Code for all religious communities was first made by the All India Women's Conference in 1937. Sixty years on, as this section will demonstrate, the demand is certainly not made by the Indian women's movement with the same confidence. By 1993, at the Northern Region Nari Mukti Sangharsh Sammelan (Women's Liberation Struggle Conference) held in Kanpur, there were two resolutions put forward for debate, one calling for a UCC, and the other for a rethinking of the notion of uniformity, given the appropriation of the demand for a UCC by the right-wing forces of the majority community. Finally, the resolution that was unanimously passed was meant to incorporate both views. And at the Fifth National Conference of Women's Studies held in Jaipur in 1995, what emerged was a broad range of positions, from the continued demand for a UCC, to outright rejection of such a move, calling instead for reform within personal laws.

In a recent interview with an Indian publication, a Bangladeshi feminist commenting on the struggle for equal laws for women expressed distress that the Indian women's movement should have shifted from its position on a Uniform Civil Code. Salma Sobhaan (1996: 5) said:

I recall extensive discussions with a wide section from within the Indian women's movement in Trivandrum in 1983 where the dominant view was a demand for a uniform civil code. At that stage I was concerned with what the emphasis on the word uniform may imply in a democracy ... Is uniformity a euphemism for majoritarian concepts dominating? ... I tried to engage many women in a dialogue about the need to look at another aspect, the identity fears and the sense of insecurity of minority groups. I was brushed aside and what each of them seemed to be saying, albeit very politely to me, was 'This is an argument that, as a Muslim, we would expect you to be making' ...

Three years later, the aftermath of the Shah Bano case[4] raised some of the questions I happened to have been making. That we should have been ... more aware, sensitive about how women feel within communities.

And now, what is the response today? Instead of a reasoning born out of such a sensitivity, I find most women's groups in India reactive and nervous, grabbing the demand for internal reforms as the proverbial last straw when faced with the systematic hysteria whipped up by fascist parties demanding a UCC ...

Are we to see this shift merely as a nervous reaction to Hindu communalism, as Sobhaan does (indeed, as many Indian feminists do)? Or does it reflect a deeper dilemma at this historical juncture for feminist politics specifically, and generally for secular, democratic politics? It might be more productive, in other words, to map the shifts in thinking on the UCC, in terms of the troubled attempts to re-engage with notions of citizenship, nation and gender.

It might also be relevant here to reflect on the significance of Sobhaan, a feminist from an 'Islamic' state with a Muslim majority population, reiterating that there continues to be a 'widespread and clearcut demand' there for a secular code, while feminists in a 'secular' Hindu majority state with rising majority community communalism seem to be rethinking such a demand. One can safely assume that if the minorities in Bangladesh resisted a common code fearing control by the majority community, the response of the Bangladeshi women's movement would reflect similar readjustments. What can such commonalities and differences suggest about the changing relationships between state, religious communities and women's movements in specific postcolonial societies?

One response to this question is what this essay seeks to trace through the story of the UCC in India. We find that the debate here is invariably set up in terms of secular state versus religious community, and has rarely surfaced in public discourse as a feminist issue. In other words, on the one hand the argument for a UCC is made in the name of protecting the integrity of the nation, which is seen to be under threat from plural systems of legality. For instance, in the Constituent Assembly, when the decision was taken to postpone the implementation of a UCC to the future by relegating it to the Directive Principles,[5] a minute of dissent to this decision was presented by three members, which put the need for a UCC in terms of 'nationhood'. It said, 'One of the factors that has kept India from advancing to nationhood has been the existence of personal laws based on religion which keeps the nation divided into watertight compartments in many aspects of life.' Clearly, 'nation' was understood to be constituted only by the dissolution of all other identities. Almost three decades later, *Towards Equality*, the report of the National Committee on the Status of Women, said:

> The absence of a UCC in the last quarter of the twentieth century, twenty-seven years after independence, is an incongruity that cannot be justified with all the emphasis that is placed on secularism, science and modernism. The continuance of various personal laws which accept discrimination between men and women violates the fundamental rights ... It is also against the spirit of national integration and secularism. (Government of India 1974: 142)

On the other hand, resistance to the UCC comes on the grounds that its implementation would destroy the cultural identities of minorities, the protection of which is crucial to democracy. This kind of argument was made both during debates in the Constituent Assembly and during the public debates over the Shah Bano judgment.

Thus while the axis upon which the UCC debate turns is gender, the public discourse around it remains poised on the polarity of state and community. Each of these categories in this context is deeply problematic for feminists.

The national integrity argument for the UCC

The state argument – that is, national integrity as the rationale for a UCC – is unacceptable for two reasons. Firstly, the explicit assumption underlying this argument is that while Hindus have willingly accepted reform, the 'other' communities continue to cling to diverse as well as retrogressive laws, threatening the integrity of the nation-state. It is misleading, though, to claim that Hindu personal law was reformed. It was merely codified, and even that was in the face of stiff resistance from Congress leaders. In fact, the proposed bill meant to overhaul laws relating to marriage and inheritance was dropped on the eve of the first general elections, but finally parts of it were pushed through later by Nehru, as the Hindu Marriage Act (1955) and the Hindu Succession Act, the Hindu Minority and Guardianship Act and the Hindu Adoption and Maintenance Act (1956).

These new Acts were by no means an unqualified advance for women's rights. On the contrary, codification put an end to the diversity of Hindu law as it was practised in different regions, in the process destroying existing, more liberal customary provisions in many cases, as for example among some communities in Rajasthan, which had easier marriage and divorce provisions. There were other ways in which the new laws made the situation worse for women. The Hindu Guardianship Act introduced the notion of the father as the 'natural guardian', which was unknown earlier, thus curtailing the rights of mothers to custody of children. Another instance is the legal recognition given to only one form of marriage ceremony practised by North Indian upper castes. As a result, bigamy in fact became easier, because if a man took another wife following any other marriage ceremony, it would not be recognised as marriage in a court, making it almost impossible for women to bring bigamous husbands to book, and affecting the rights of both women. There was a limited improvement in women's rights to property, but women are still not co-partners in family property, while in matrilineal systems the notion of equal rights of sons and daughters to property was used to give men rights to inherit which they did not have under the traditional system.

The second, more fundamental problem with the national integrity argument emerges from the first point – from the recognition of the homogenising thrust of the Hindu Code. The rejection of practices and lifestyles which did not conform to a particular North Indian, upper-caste construction of the family was justified on the grounds that these other practices were not 'Indian'. This entity of the 'nation' is constructed only through the marginalisation and exclusion of a multiplicity of other interests and identities.

The community argument against the UCC

At the same time, feminists cannot accept the unqualified rights of communities to their cultural identity, although providing space for such identity is crucial for a democratic polity. For one thing, the 'community' identity that is claimed today as natural and prior to all other identity is no more primordial than the nation is. Communities are constituted in particular ways at different historical junctures, but the process of their formation is naturalised at each stage. It seems, therefore, that no other way of being had ever been possible. However, a rich and complex debate among historians has begun to explore the alternative possibilities that existed in eighteenth- and nineteenth-century India. At the risk of flattening the contours of this debate, I will broadly sketch the two major positions in order to unpack the notion of 'community'.

One kind of argument holds that the 'religious community' was produced by the colonial censuses and other official enumerations of the late nineteenth century. People who lived in premodern social forms, while they had a strong sense of community, did not define themselves primarily in terms of their difference from other groups, and did not perceive themselves as belonging to only particular communities. It was the mechanisms of modern governance introduced through colonial rule that reconstituted the meaning of community along the lines primarily of religion, sharpening the previously 'fuzzy' boundaries of overlapping community identities.

In other words, the logic of modern competitive politics was such that people came to fit the categories that colonial authorities fashioned for them. Dipesh Chakrabarty (1995: 3377) goes so far as to argue that these identities in contemporary India are based on religious categories as a result of the reification of 'religious identity' by the British. Had the British picked language as a criterion of community demarcation, he believes the result would have been that different language groups would have had the sense of identity which religious groups have today.

The position counter to this says that colonial authority was not the exclusive source of community identities as they are constituted today. Rather, a 'critical public' was already in place in India, as C.A. Bayly (1994: 9) for example, argues. This public was the body of intelligentsia and administrators who represented the views of the populace to the rulers from the late Mughal rule onwards. Thus, this argument emphasises that the indigenous domain of social and political critique had agency in constituting identities of various sorts. That is, the colonial state only took over, and took further, existing ways of constituting the self. In other words, community identity as it exists today is only partly shaped by colonial intervention, and reflects a process of development that goes back much further.

For the purposes of our present discussion it is not necessary to enter into this debate. I emphasise one point only as relevant here – the recognition of the historicity and constructedness of identity. Particularly, we need to recognise the role played by the emergence of the modern 'public sphere' in the formation of community identity. With the creation of this sphere, multiple experiences of constituting the 'self' were gradually subsumed into sharply defined and internally homogeneous identities, the only identities acceptable to the rules of modern governance.

Warren Hastings's regulation of 1772 laid the foundations of the courts of the East India Company and, through them, the logic of fixing identities into rigid categories. The regulation provided that in certain matters, such as those concerning succession, marriage, caste and religious institutions, Hindus and Muslims would be ruled by their respective laws, while no such uniform laws for entire communities existed. As a result, what the British judges recognised as authentic was 'sastric' law for Hindus and interpretation by a Kadi in the case of Muslims. Even in accepting that in cases where customary practices differed from 'scriptural law' custom was to prevail, the British began to fix as law any custom that was proved. This was then imposed on similar cases in the future. Thus the law was gradually transformed from being a vast body of texts and locally variegated customs, all of which was constantly interpreted, to a rigid, codified body of legal rules – the personal laws. In other words, the personal laws being defended in the name of religious 'tradition' are constructions of the nineteenth and twentieth centuries.

However, recognising the historical process by which communities came into being, while challenging their claim to a 'natural' and primordial essence, does not deny the 'reality' of these identities in contemporary times. Nevertheless, even while accepting this reality, feminists need to reject community identity as an overriding one for other reasons. Rights claimed by communities vis-à-vis the state – autonomy, selfhood, access to resources – are denied by communities to 'their' women. The personal laws of all communities discriminate against women in terms of rights to property, both in the natal family and within marriage, rights within marriage and upon divorce, and rights to custody of children. In other words, the discriminatory provisions of the personal laws are based on the same logic of exclusions that characterises the national integrity argument which seeks to delegitimise separate personal laws, and must be rejected on the same grounds.

The women's movement and the UCC debate

The response of the women's movement to the UCC has taken different forms over the last five decades. From the 1950s to the mid-1980s, there was general consensus that the state be held accountable for upholding the fundamental right to equality, and should therefore be pushed to legislate a gender-just civil code applicable to all communities. This position was never consciously articulated as distinct from the mainstream discourse of national integration. The two aims of gender justice and national integration seemed to be part of the same project. Flavia Agnes (1994: 1125) has argued that the distinction between the two was never made adequately clear by the women's movement because 'Although most of the initiators of the movement were culturally Hindu, they perceived themselves as secular beings.' As a result the movement did not focus on the Hindu Code, which was understood to have been reformed, while it would rally around important cases brought by minority women challenging their personal laws

While there is some truth to Agnes's explanation, it might be more accurate to understand differently the apparent conflation of national integrity with gender justice in that period. That is, the conflation does not reflect the incomplete secularisation of feminist activists, but rather reflects the relationship of the women's movement with the idea of the nation-state. Until the mid-1960s, the legitimacy of the post-independence elites ensured an ebb in the militancy of social movements. The women's movement settled down to cooperate with the state in development programmes and gradual institutionalisation. The rhetoric of national integrity continued to have currency not just for the women's movement, but for other social movements too, because the nation had the legitimacy of having been so recently carved out through a mass struggle encompassing different currents. In addition, an inevitable hangover from the anti-imperialist struggle was the characterisation of the state as an ally in progressive transformation.

However, by the mid-1970s, the legitimacy of the post-independence elites had begun to erode, with the economic and political crisis precipitated by the failure of development planning. There was a resurgence of militancy in every section of society. Political repression followed, through the imposition of internal emergency by Indira Gandhi's government in 1975. This repression led to mass discontent, culminating in the lifting of the emergency in 1977. From this period there was renewed political activity in the women's movement, in what is called its 'second wave', with middle- and working-class women participating in greater and greater numbers in alternative development activities and mass struggles on every front.

This phase also marks the beginning of rethinking in the women's movement over the legitimacy of the national integrity argument. Particularly with the Shah Bano judgment in 1985 and the political campaigns that developed around it, and the growing presence of organised Hindu communalism, feminist forces found it necessary to gradually rethink the demand for a UCC. They were forced to recognise the appropriation of this issue by the Bharatiya Janata Party and Hindu communalist forces in general, which characterised the Muslim community's resistance to the UCC as its inability to integrate into the nation.

Indeed, such an understanding marks not only Hindu communal arguments but even judicial pronouncements. The Shah Bano judgment itself, as well as other more recent judgments on Muslim personal law – the Allahabad High Court judgment on triple *talaq* (1994) and the Supreme Court judgment in the Sarla Mudgal case (1995) – makes explicit the argument that Hindus have willingly accepted reform while 'other' communities continue to cling to diverse and retrogressive laws, threatening the integrity of the nation-state. The 1995 judgment said, for example, that 'In the Indian Republic, there was to be only one nation, the Indian nation, and no community could claim to remain a separate entity on the basis of religion.' As the Women's Research and Action Group stated in 1995, 'Why did the judiciary consistently raise the demand for a UCC only in the context of cases dealing with Muslim Personal Law, and never in dealing with cases of discrimination in Hindu Law?' In other words, the judiciary seems to share the assumption of the Hindu right-wing that Hindu law has been satisfactorily reformed, and that a UCC is necessary only to redress inequalities in Muslim laws.

By the time of the Shah Bano judgment, it was clear that in every way the nation was constituted by dominant discourses, the powerless and the marginal were being defined out of its boundaries. National integrity could no longer be a value the women's movement could subscribe to unconditionally. This recognition, along with discomfort over the routine invocation of the 'integrity of the nation' mantra in order to castigate minority communities as 'anti-national', gradually brought about in feminist thinking on the UCC an explicit detaching of the national integrity argument from the gender justice argument.

This shift is reflected in work that re-examined the Hindu personal law and argued that it was not reformed but merely codified, and that this codification put an end to the diversity of Hindu law as it was practised in different regions. The process destroyed more liberal customary provisions for women in many cases. Other work examined the ways in which secular legislation like the Special Marriage Act was amended to protect the property rights of Hindu men, thus dispelling the myth that only men of minority communities benefited from the lack of a UCC.

Thus, in the last decade, feminist critiques of the inequality of personal laws have come to distinguish themselves from national integrity arguments for a UCC. On the other hand, feminist critiques of authoritarian state power have tried explicitly to demarcate themselves from the unqualified defence of 'community rights'.

Current feminist positions on the UCC

In this section I will outline the major responses to the UCC that have emerged in the last few years from women's groups and other democratic platforms. Broadly, five kinds of positions have emerged.

1. Compulsory common code

Saheli and People's Union for Democratic Rights of Delhi argue that we should not be intimidated by the communalisation of the polity brought about by the politics of Hindutva. Feminist and democratic politics requires that we reaffirm our commitment to equal rights for women across communities, particularly in the face of patriarchal resistance from all quarters. Saheli's position is that we should continue to make our demand for a common gender-just code, differentiating it clearly from the agenda of the Hindu right. This argument is that plurality of laws creates conflicts and works against the interests of women (as in the Shah Bano case for example, where the common criminal law provision was overridden by the Muslim personal law). Our struggle therefore must be for a compulsory common code which would override personal laws, all of which discriminate against women, and defend this discrimination in the name of religious freedom.

2. Reforms from within

Here, the argument is that any all-encompassing code, whether propounded by the Hindu right or based on feminist understandings, will harm the interests of women from minority communities, since in today's sharply communalised politics, they bear the double burden of being a minority and being women. Efforts to bring about gender justice, therefore, must focus primarily on strengthening initiatives to bring about reforms in personal laws, so that the rights of women do not become a casualty of the fear of minority communities.

Within this position there are two main strands:

(a) Muslim and Christian groups working on the reform of their respective personal laws, such as Nikahnama Group and Women's Research and Action Group (WRAG), both from Bombay, and Joint Women's Programme, an all-India front of Christian groups, feel that women in the community are not willing to respond to changes that come from outside the community, or which seem to threaten community identity. WRAG, in fact, has conducted a countrywide survey in which it interviewed 15 000 Muslim women, as well as lawyers, judges, social and political activists and religious leaders. Preliminary results indicate that differences in practices are very evident from one part of the country to another and so are the sources from which the practices derive. WRAG argues, therefore, that there is potential within this diversity for more radical interpretations of texts and customary practices. The Christian groups, similarly, claim to draw on the more egalitarian New Testament rather than the Old Testament on which the Christian Marriage Act of 1872 is based. All these groups agree there is no scope within this framework for gender justice in a feminist sense. However, in their opinion, the only practicable alternative at the present moment is to focus on smaller changes which will provide more rights for women even if they do not measure up to absolute gender justice.

Other women's groups which do not work with particular communities have also expressed apprehensions about enacting uniform laws. Vimochana, a group from Bangalore, feels that formal court structures are inimical to women, and favours community-based informal arbitration forums. Similarly, other groups like Anveshi from Hyderabad and Sanchetana from Ahmedabad strongly advocate initiatives for reforms from within the community, to transform the personal laws in more egalitarian and less discriminatory directions. Such initiatives, they believe, will be more acceptable to the communities than intervention by the state.

(b) Imtiaz Ahmad, who has also been involved in the mobilisation of democratic opinion within the Muslim community, provides the second strand of the 'reform from within' school of thought (1995: 2851–2). Ahmad makes his argument in the context of two principles: 'external protection', that is, the right of communities to preserve their identity within the larger collectivity of the nation-state, and 'internal restriction', or prohibitions upon the power of communities to deny to sections of their members rights to which they are entitled as citizens. The first would require the state to ensure that no law or any societal force would interfere in the ability of groups to preserve their cultural or religious identity. The second would place upon the community itself the responsibility to ensure that no section inside it would be deprived of the rights that other citizens of the state enjoyed.

Ahmad feels that the enactment of any common code is problematic. First, it is not clear what the contours of such a code would be – whether it would be limited to issues of inheritance, marriage and divorce, as the debates on the UCC seem to suggest, or whether it would cover other aspects of the law as well, including provisions like the Hindu Undivided Family Tax, which offers tax benefits only to the Hindu community. Of course, by this argument Ahmad is suggesting that the Hindu right wing is making only a selective argument for the UCC. Second, the legal diversities in the country are so great that any attempt to enact a common code would generate widespread resentment among communities forced to give up their ways of life. Third, the existing laws are founded on at least four clearly distinct jurisprudential philosophies – Anglican, Hindu, Muslim and tribal. The principle for the reconciliation of all these philosophies, an essential prerequisite for the formulation of a UCC, has not yet been thought about. Finally, Ahmad concludes, personal laws of some communities, particularly tribal communties such as the Nagas and Mizos, enjoy constitutional protection. Enactment of a UCC would entail constitutional amendments which would not be readily acceptable to these communities.

The appropriate strategy in this situation, Ahmad argues, is for communities themselves to rationalise those aspects of their personal laws which are in conflict with constitutional provisions for equality, or which may not be in the Constitution but which nevertheless fail to pass the test of equity, justice and good conscience. This course of action would be in keeping with the principles Ahmad has outlined: (a) external protection of the democratic rights of communities *vis-à-vis* the larger society, that is, no imposition of a UCC by the state, and (b) internal restrictions imposed by themselves to ensure the rights of sections of their own population.

3. Legislation on areas not covered by personal laws

By confining legislation for the present to areas not covered by personal laws, some groups hope to bring about gender justice without directly confronting community pressure. This is a formulation which presents aspects of both the positions discussed above, and is provided by Majlis from Bombay and the All India Democratic Women's Association (AIDWA), the women's wing of the Communist Party of India (Marxist).

Majlis (1996) points out that the UCC has become synonymous in the public mind with reform of barbaric Islamic customs. The focus is never on the protection of economic rights of women within marriage and upon divorce, but rather on polygamy and triple *talaq*, thus targeting the Muslim community alone. Further, Majlis contends that, given our limited exposure to customs and practices in a diverse and multicultural society like India, we are not in a position to work out legal principles for an encompassing code. Majlis warns that more harm than good can come out of the destruction of safeguards which are built within the community. Recognising the need for law reform, however, Majlis suggests that along with support for reform initiatives within communities, feminists should work towards smaller, specific and focused statutes which will address some of the immediate problems faced by women, particularly in the areas of domestic violence and economic rights. Since these areas do not fall within personal laws, there will be no room to communalise the issue, and at the same time this will protect the rights of women by addressing their immediate problems within marriage.

AIDWA, while affirming its commitment to 'Equal Rights, Equal Laws' at its national convention in December 1995, advocates a step-by-step approach which is similar to the strategy suggested by Majlis. It has reiterated the need for common laws based on equality for all women, in every sphere, economic, social, political and legal. However, rather than advocating any state legislation across the board, it suggests the strengthening of the common legal ground for women by enacting laws in specific areas. These areas are rights to property acquired after marriage, registration of marriages regardless of the religious rituals followed, and domestic violence. AIDWA sees immediate reform possible only in areas which do not directly conflict with existing personal laws. Its analysis of the present political landscape appears, therefore, to be similar to that of the positions advocating reform from within, although this is never explicitly stated.

4. Optional gender-just code

This position holds that since it is not clear what a common code would look like the first imperative is that the feminist and democratic forces evolve a model of such a code based on the experience of the women's movement in India and elsewhere. Once this gender-just code is put into place, personal laws would ordinarily prevail, but in times of dispute women would have the choice of opting for this code, which would ensure their rights better than personal laws would.

One group which has evolved such a code is the Forum Against the Oppression of Women, in Bombay. It has invited other women's groups to debate the code in order to begin the process. One of the highlights of the Forum's proposal is the broadening of the concept of the family to include homosexual relationships and people living together outside marriage, so as to ensure the protection of the rights of the women living in them. Thus, the Forum's proposal would ensure the bigamist's responsibility to his first wife, but not at the cost of the second woman.

5. Reverse optionality

The proposal of reverse optionality has been put forward by the Working Group on Women's Rights (WGWR) of Delhi, which hopes, through this device, to break through the impasse created by the polarisations of state–community and community–women. WGWR critiques demands that have so far been put forward for a UCC on the grounds that such demands have either explicitly foregrounded national integrity or have been appropriated for that idea, rather than being based on gender justice. On the other hand, reform from within personal laws has been blocked by patriarchal pressures within communities. So while supporting all feminist initiatives for reforms from within, WGWR feels this would be a limited strategy.

WGWR's proposal has three planks:

(1) The preparation and institutionalisation of a comprehensive gender-just package of legislation which will cover equal rights for women not only within the family but in the sphere of work as well (e.g. crèches, equal wages, etc.).

(2) All citizens of India would be covered by this framework of common law at birth or upon taking citizenship.

(3) All citizens would have the right to choose to be governed by personal laws if they desire, while retaining the option to revoke this choice at some future date, in order to return to their birthright of secular laws.

This proposal reverses the present situation where people are born into personal laws and have to make a decision to opt for the few secular laws which exist in the area covered by personal laws. This decision is more difficult for women to make under the present circumstances, but if gender-just laws are their birthright, their interests would be better protected.

A broad consensus has emerged among feminist groups on the lines of action to be taken in future, that there are three broad areas from which it is possible to devise a common agenda. Women's groups need to support initiatives for reform within personal laws and work towards ensuring the passage of already formulated reforms which are held up, such as the reforms to Christian law. At the same time, work is required towards the formulation of legislation on areas where laws do not exist. Such areas need to be identified, as well as what the content of these laws should be.

In the long term, women's groups should work together to evolve the specific content of a comprehensive gender-just package of legislation. This is crucial, in order to move forward on the question of women's rights, as well as to counter any programme the BJP might put forward. Whether we argue that such a gender-just package is to be brought about all at once or in stages, this is the moment for elaborating its content definitively.

There remain, however, misgivings about the very exercise of drafting laws. In May 1996, on the eve of the general elections, a group called Human Rights Law Network decided to organise a workshop in Bombay in order to draft a gender-just family code, apparently to pre-empt a possible BJP government from taking the initiative. In response, a letter was circulated to women's groups and to the organisers of the workshop by fifteen of the groups or individuals who had been invited, expressing concern at the 'premature' haste with which a common family code was being created. The letter explained their concern in terms of the situation in Maharashtra after Hindu right-wing parties were elected to government there a year previously. The BJP Shiv Sena government had carried out a number of actions targeting the Muslim community. It dissolved the Minorities Commission, banned cow slaughter and disbanded the Srikrishna Commission, which was in the process of conducting an inquiry into the pogrom against Muslims in Bombay in 1992–3. The state government had also passed a Bill prohibiting polygamy. The letter went on to say, 'We feel very strongly against offering the present state more power of intervention in the life of marginalised communities.' Further, it pointed out that the BJP is at present the only political party demanding a UCC, and the existence of a concrete draft would only strengthen the hands of a BJP government should it come to power. The letter concluded that the focus of the workshop should be shifted from 'drafting laws' to 'discussing strategies'.

Mapping the shifts, I: The move away from uniformity

It is significant that the term 'uniform' has been dropped altogether as a positive value from the debates within the movement, even by the positions which re-iterate the need for state legislation. Whether like Saheli and People's Union for Democratic Rights they advocate a compulsory code, or like Forum Against Oppression of Women an optional code, or like the Working Group on Women's Rights a negotiable common code, all use the terms 'common', 'gender-just' or 'egalitarian' instead of 'uniform'.

Here it is significant that of all the groups discussed, the one with the longest history, the All India Democratic Women's Association, also displays the sharpest shift in position over these decades. As the women's wing of the Communist Party of India (Marxist), it had uncompromisingly stood for the need for common laws for all communities. Now, while not explicitly adopting the kind of critique of a common code offered by Majlis, WRAG or the Nikahnama Group, AIDWA evidently does not feel that the time is ripe for such a code. It advocates instead, as we have seen, a step-by-step approach – legislation on areas not covered by personal laws, and simultaneously support of initiatives for reform within communities. AIDWA goes further in urging, not just support for initiatives towards personal law reform, but also struggle for such reform. AIDWA contends that feminists have surrendered the arena of personal laws to patriarchal forces, and stresses the need to recover our agency here.

This is significant because the women's movement by and large, and particularly the AIDWA, has tended to consider personal laws as being beyond recovery from a feminist point of view, based as they are on claims to religious traditions. If AIDWA now feels it necessary to launch a campaign in this area, then clearly a radical rethinking has come about.

This overall disavowal of uniformity marks an implicit recognition, I suggest, of the fact that although the Hindu right-wing appears to assert particularity by bringing religious identity into the realm of the state, its claim is rather that the state has reneged on the promise of uniformity – it has not truly protected the abstract citizen, unmarked by religion. The Hindu right claims that secularism has meant in practice that the majority community has had to surrender its interests while the state has protected those of minorities. In other words, the argument is that the state has not delivered on its promise of abstract citizenship – minorities have retained their personal laws, the only Muslim-majority state of Kashmir has a special status within the framework of the constitution, and so on. Secular critiques have seen Hindu communalism as threatening the abstract citizen enshrined in the Constitution with its assertion of Hinduness. I argue rather that in this context, secular discourse and Hindu communal discourse occupy the same terrain – that of claiming to be the true protectors of the rights of the abstract citizen.

In their study of the Hindu right, Tapan Basu *et al.* (1993: 76–7) establish that within the imagined Hindu *rashtra* (nation), the Muslim is first declared a free and equal citizen and the *rashtra* is defined in secular terms as the community that resides on a particular piece of land. After this first step, however, the land is sacralised through a 'Hinduisation' of its geographical and historical features, so that the Muslim can be a citizen only on the terms set by Hinduism. Further, the Hinduism that emerges is one that is invested with all the known marks of orthodox Brahminical piety.

This process of defining Hindu *rashtra* is no different from the nationalist process of defining a secular India. Here the status of citizen is offered to all those who fulfil the conditions of birth or lineage within the national boundaries, regardless of other affiliations. In the next move, this formal equality is qualified by factors like religion and gender in so far as religious codes govern women's rights in the family, or by class in so far as the right to work does not exist in the Constitution.

I suggest that it is in disavowal of this homogenising thrust of both the nation-state and of Hindu right-wing politics that even those within the women's movement who continue to advocate state legislation have come to stake out their position so differently, moving away from the notion of uniformity altogether. The state no longer has the legitimacy it once had as an ally in progressive transformation, and the women's movement has come to recognise the disempowering implications of uniformity, whether of the communal or secular variety.

Mapping the shifts, II: Reasserting citizenship

At the same time as they reject uniformity, all the responses implicitly or explicitly prioritise the notion of women as individual citizens invested with inalienable rights. Even the positions which contend that at present reform within personal laws is preferable to legislation by the state are not really asserting the rights of communities over those of individuals. Rather, these are attempts to negotiate the maximum space for women as individuals within their communities, given the communalised situation which threatens minority community identity.

The debate continues, but what is significant is that this intense self-questioning reflects a radical rethinking of one of the givens of democratic politics in India, that a 'secular' state has a mandate to bring about progressive social transformation. Here it might be useful to consider Mahmood Mamdani's characterisation of 'modernists' in Africa as those who see 'civil society' as the space for democratisation. 'Central to [the current Africanist discourse on civil society] are two claims: civil society exists as a fully formed construct in Africa as in Europe, and the driving force of democratization everywhere is the contention between civil society and the state' (1996: 13–14).

However, our discussion of the UCC debate in India suggests that here the modernists have seen the task of creating a civil society itself as the responsibility of the state. In other words, through legislation and administrative measures, the state has been expected to intervene into 'non-modern' spaces to bring about equality. It is this conviction that has come increasingly to be questioned, not just by critics of modernity, but by modernists as well. In the range of feminist positions on the UCC debate, the arguments advocating reforms within communities as preferable to state intervention represent a civil society argument in the making. As we have seen, these arguments are not made in 'traditional' or communitarian terms, but very much in the modernist language of citizenship. That is, all the positions outlined above, even when they reject a common civil code altogether, do not defend 'tradition' as opposed to 'modernity' but, rather, urge reform of personal laws in keeping with principles of citizenship and equality. These two tendencies – the rejection of uniformity and the reassertion of citizenship – reveal a strong tension which I would argue is characteristic of social movements of the late twentieth century.

The paradox of constitutionality

The politics of these movements express simultaneously (a) the need to move away from 'uniformity' and homogenisation, and the statism implied by these terms, and (b) the reassertion of citizenship as a category which continues to have resonance for emancipatory politics. To put it another way, this tension can be seen as one in which the need to assert specific moral visions comes up against the drive of constitutionality and its language of universal rights. We need to historicise the emergence of the language of rights. The idea of individuals as bearers of rights is barely four hundred years old. These centuries have seen the expansion of democratic rights to more and more sections of the people, and the discourse of rights has empowered social movements of different kinds. In the movement from feudal communitarianism to bourgeois individualism, this discourse certainly freed the individual from the circumscription of feudal hierarchies. But the notion of the citizen empowered with rights in the public sphere derived its emancipatory potential precisely from its positioning against feudal absolutism. With the completion of the bourgeois revolution in the West, and the mediated and refracted way in which this transformation takes place in colonial and post-colonial societies, the language of rights has lost its relevance.

Over the centuries, this language has been extended from rights of the individual against the state, to rights of collectivities against one other as well as against individuals. Rights have come to be defined in such broad terms as 'the right to be fully human', as Charles Taylor (1986) puts it. And in these new forms, rights are to be guaranteed by the state, which is a long journey to have travelled from the original notion of rights as capacities which individuals held against the state. The contradictions raised by this journey have so far been inadequately confronted.

Rights claims are made on the assumption that rights are self-evident, universally comprehended and universally applicable. But in fact, the validity of rights claims for those who make them derives from a universe of shared memory within a delimited community, whether of feminists or ethnic or any other groups. Indeed, the political task is precisely to construct such a universe of particular, shared moral visions of the past and future. Rights claims derive their meaning only within their specific universes. Yet rights continue to have no other language to be expressed in except the language of constitutionality and law, the force of which is towards uniformity. This language requires universally applied principles, while rights, which are used to enter the arena of law, are constituted differently by different discourses. Consequently, there is an inevitable slippage of meaning once rights enter the legal arena, where diverse discourses of rights converge.

The fixity of meaning required by legal discourse has generated a dilemma for feminists. This has come to be formulated as difference-versus-sameness. When 'equality before the law' is interpreted as men and women being the same as each other, courts do not uphold any legislation intended either to compensate for past discrimination or to take into account gender-specific differences like maternity. Thus the sameness approach cannot differentiate between 'differential treatment that disadvantages and differential treatment that advantages', as Cossman and Kapur (1996: 20–1) put it. Liberal feminists who subscribe to the sameness approach continue to insist, however, that the only way for women to achieve legal recognition of their equal status to men is to deny the legal relevance of their difference to the degree that it exists. Women should be recognised, in this view, as gender-neutral legal persons.

The opposing position from within feminism is that this accepts the masculine as the norm, and prevents the visibilty of the unique experience of women. However, the difference approach in law has at best been protectionist, thus denying women the claim to equality altogether. It has also been used by courts to justify discriminatory treatment on the grounds that women are different from men. Thus feminists seeking justice through the law have come up against the limits set by the criterion that law be uniform and consistent. It can either recognise sameness (which disadvantages women) or difference (which justifies discrimination). Attempts to transcend this divide through notions like 'substantive equality' are only possible by asserting feminist ideals as universal ideals, which clearly they are not. The substantive model requires that in some contexts the sameness approach should be used, and in others the difference approach. However, if the reasoning underlying substantive equality could simply be implemented through the sensitisation of judges, if the morality driving that reasoning were so unthreatening to the dominant social order, we would not need the law to bring about social justice.

It seems clear therefore that rights are constituted by values derived from specific moral universes, There is, in other words, a singularity to justice, a uniqueness which is at odds with law, which must take a more general form, as Law and as Rule. At particular historical moments, 'justice' is constituted by a plurality of moral visions, but the discourse of law must fix meaning in determinate ways. The meaning delivered as the 'just' one then gets articulated in complex ways with other discourses constituting identity, and tends to sediment dominant and oppressive possibilities rather than marginal and emancipatory ones.

I would like to illustrate this argument with the consideration of a recent case pertaining to the UCC debate. In 1994, the Allahabad High Court held that a customary divorce, either under the Shariat Law or the Hindu Marriage Act, is not valid if it violates the principle of equality in the Constitution. In this instance, triple *talaq* as a method of divorce was held to be discriminatory to women, and the divorce of a Muslim couple in the case was held to be invalid. The point to be noted is that this was not a case regarding the validity of *talaq* at all. Rather, it arose from two writ petitions from a divorced couple challenging the clubbing together of their lands for the purposes of the Land Ceiling Act. They claimed that they had divorced in 1969, and so the wife was entitled to hold land separately in her own name. The judge held that the oral divorce was invalid, despite the existence of witnesses and a valid *talaqnama* or papers of divorce. As a result, what appears to be a judgment upholding the rights of women in fact deprives the woman, in this case, of the right to own property in her own name.

The conflict here is between land reform legislation and women's rights to own land, both of which rest on the same principle of equity. The latter are often overridden in an attempt by the state to prevent the circumventing of land ceiling regulations through the classification of land as separately owned by different members of the family. This contradiction was most evident in Kerala where matrilineal property arrangements had obtained among some communities – the Communist Ministry's land reform measures of the 1950s dealt the death blow to land rights that women had traditionally held. The ideological device which operates to iron out the contradiction between social justice through land reforms and individual rights of women to property is the institution of marriage, by which a 'couple' is created, within which the woman is subsumed. However, the solution is not to simply separate out the individuals within the family as 'citizens' – that would in this instance only perpetuate property inequalities between individuals of different classes. A simple privileging of 'universal rights of the citizen', therefore, cannot help democratic movements to negotiate conflicts among equally important universal rights.

Ebrahim Moosa argues in his essay in this volume that the Constitution of South Africa, while invoking God and Religion, in fact fails to embody a normative ethical vision specific to African traditions. I contend that this is characteristic of the drive of constitutionality in general. Its thrust is towards the erasure of any kind of normative ethic which differs from its own unitary central ethic. Precisely in such a denial of subjective ethics lay its emancipatory potential at one time, the moment of transition from feudalism to capitalism. That moment has passed. This is particularly evident at this historical moment, when democratic aspirations are not simply counterposed to an absolutist state but are articulated in much more complex ways, as we have seen.

And yet the notion of full citizenship guaranteed by a constitution continues to have a moral strength which social movements for democracy continue to draw upon. It is this irreconcilable, nevertheless productive, tension which is reflected in the diversity and unrecognisability of movements for democratisation. Is it possible to relocate rights into a language other than the one that they have been assigned? Perhaps such a dislocation would enable us to recapture the notion of politics as critique, rather than as merely seeking space within already defined boundaries of power.

To illustrate this possibility, let us go back briefly to the discussion on the UCC in India. Where, in all the discussion and contestation among feminist positions, is a reflection of feminist critiques of the family as an oppressive and normalising institution? On the contrary, what we find ourselves engaged in is the constant reassertion of the heterosexual, monogamous marriage as the norm. In our efforts to address the injustice women face within personal laws, we seem to have moved further and further on the path of legitimising state regulation of forms of human interaction and intimacy. In order to recapture the emancipatory potential of the notion of the rights-bearing citizen, it seems we may need to relocate it from the realm of law and the state. This would render it unrecognisable in many ways – we have a very different kind or kinds of struggles ahead.

Chapter Five

Religious revivalism, human rights activism and the struggle for women's rights in Nigeria

Hussaina J Abdullah

The period from the mid-1980s in Nigeria has witnessed the emergence of three apparently parallel but ultimately related trends that have become important defining elements of the contemporary socio-political and cultural landscape of the country. The first has to do with the emergence and flowering of a host of associations specifically dedicated to the promotion and defence of human rights, civil liberties and legal and constitutional reform. Between 1987, when the Civil Liberties Organisation (CLO) was founded, and 1995, at least thirty other such groups were established in different parts of the country. The second trend centres on an unmistakable religious revivalism entailing the revitalisation of many existing religious (essentially Christian and Muslim) structures and networks and, perhaps more significantly, the rapid growth of (North American-type) pentecostalist and spiritualist churches and 'fundamentalist' activist Islamic organisations. The third trend is connected with the explicit expansion of interest from above (at the level of the state) and from below (at the level of civil society) in the promotion of women's rights and interests.

In so far as the state's interest in women is concerned, it has been described elsewhere as signalling the emergence of 'state feminism' and a process of 'femocracy' linked to the 'First Lady' phenomenon that is rapidly gaining ground in Africa, sometimes with the support of 'developmentally'-oriented United Nations (UN) agencies like the United Nations Children's Emergency Fund (UNICEF) and the United Nations Development Programme (UNDP) (Abdullah 1994, 1995). As to the promotion of women's rights at the societal level, a host of nongovernmental groups has been formed or revived which are explicitly devoted to the promotion of political, legal, cultural and intellectual activism in support of Nigerian women.

These three trends, which have emerged to define the contemporary Nigerian landscape, have unfolded within the conditioning context of two important factors. The first of these centres on the prolonged national economic crisis which started in 1981 and which has not been mitigated (some would even argue has been complicated) by the neo-liberal economic Structural Adjustment Programme adopted in 1987 with IMF–World Bank support to contain it. The second factor relates to the deepening crisis of governance and legitimisation most vividly captured by the continuing subjection of the country to progressively worsening forms of military despotism. Both of these factors, in providing the context for the emergence of the three trends referred to earlier, also provide the bases for the interconnection between them.

The deep-seated crisis in the national economy has not only resulted in the collapse of real incomes for most Nigerians and a sharp decline in social citizenship, as state-supported social services went into decay on account of the fiscal and governance problems confronting the country; it has also provided fertile ground for political authoritarianism and militarism to thrive. A perceptible loss of faith in secular authorities has gone side by side with the rise of religious fundamentalism; the collapse in personal and household incomes has been accompanied by the growth of the prosperity gospel; economic decline and political dictatorship, as well as the violation of rights associated with them, have fuelled popular concern about the protection of human rights and political liberties. The intensification of corruption among state officials, amidst the popular disenfranchisement occasioned by economic decline and political authoritarianism, has eroded the legitimacy of the state and alienated many from state politics.

Economic crisis, structural adjustment and political authoritarianism have been central to the transformation of popular identities in contemporary Nigeria. Shifts in the balance of social forces, most of which have been to the detriment of the working poor and the old class of professionals, have not only created a crisis of identities but also spurred activism at the level of religious practices and rights advocacy, as individuals and groups attempt to make sense of national decline, protect themselves against its worst effects, and reassert their place and relevance as members of the polity.

This essay is concerned to assess the implications of the growth of human rights and civil liberties activism, side by side with a simultaneous process of religious revivalism and a rising and institutionalised 'state feminism', for the autonomous struggle from below for the protection and advancement of the rights of Nigerian women. It entails an evaluation of the extent to which the concerns and struggles of Nigerian women have been built into the programmes and activities of the growing human rights and civil liberties community, and of the ways in which activist women's organisations have themselves sought to anchor and deepen the campaign for women's rights amidst the pressures posed by the new 'religiosity' in the country and the authoritarian impulse associated with 'state feminism'.

At one level, the struggles of activist women's organisations have involved the articulation of strategies for responding to the de-politicising thrust and consequences of 'state feminism'/'femocracy', whilst simultaneously attempting to tap potentially positive elements from the process for the benefit of Nigerian women. At another level, they have entailed the broadening of the campaign for women's concerns and rights with regard to issues of legal and constitutional reform. International networking with other women's groups has also been employed as a strategy for advancing the interests of Nigerian women, especially as they pertain to the Convention on the Elimination of Discrimination Against Women (CEDAW).

Furthermore, there has been an attempt by some women's groups to use the idiom of religion and contestations over doctrinal interpretation to press the case for reforms. In this regard, the experience of the Federation of Muslim Women's Associations in Nigeria (FOMWAN) will be used as a specific case study to show the possibilities and limitations of this specific approach. For the struggles of Nigerian women for reform and change still have to contend with resilient patriarchal structures, which aspects of religious revivalism have tended to reinforce. Of particular concern are certain discriminatory practices against women and daily expressions of gender inequality which the dominant religions tend to justify through their doctrines. The explosion of human rights activism has, so far, been insufficient to challenge significantly the structures of patriarchy. Some of the intellectual and policy challenges posed by this situation will inform the concluding part of this study.

The emergence of contemporary social movements in Nigeria in the 1980s

In many respects, the human rights and civil liberties associations, establishment and women's activist groups, and radical or spiritualist religious organisations that emerged or were revived in Nigeria during the 1980s were the products of a process that, in its remote origins, can be dated to the 1970s. Following the end of the Nigerian Civil War (1967–1970), the country was, in the course of the 1970s, propelled into an era of unprecedented social and economic expansion which was underpinned by rapidly growing petro-dollar revenues from oil exports. The huge petro-dollar windfall that accrued to the country was made possible by the OPEC oil price increases of 1973 and 1977–8. The revenues, averaging some US$12 billion annually for much of the decade of the 1970s, were applied by succeeding governments partly to finance the reconstruction and rehabilitation of the national economy generally and the war-torn areas in particular, and partly to expand the country's physical and social infrastructure, including the supply of modern health and educational services. But a substantial part of the revenues also fed into the 'primitive' accumulation strategies of the Nigerian elite, so much so that 'corruption' or the 'ten per cent' culture became almost integral to the socio-economic policies, programmes and practices of the state.

By the mid-1970s, the Nigerian economy began decisively to take on the character of a 'monocultural' economy, with oil increasingly accounting for a disproportionate share of the national revenues. By the end of the 1970s, the country had come to depend on oil exports for over 90 per cent of its total revenues and foreign exchange receipts (Olukoshi 1993). This was in spite of the routine proclamations made by succeeding regimes, military and civilian, that the diversification of the country's economic base was a matter of national priority. The failure to achieve this objective, therefore, meant that the country was extremely vulnerable to any adverse development in the world oil market. Not surprisingly, the Nigerian government was neither prepared for nor able immediately to cope with the sudden collapse of the world oil market in the early 1980s. The collapse of the world market price of oil from a high of US$42 at the end of the 1970s, to below US$10 at one point during the 1980s, translated into a revenue collapse for the Nigerian state. Given the heavily import-dependent nature of the economy, a major balance of payments and external debt crisis became almost inevitable. Nigeria was, therefore, ushered inexorably into a deep-seated recession from which it has still not recovered.

To stem the tide of economic decline, and the social decay that accompanied it, succeeding governments adopted different austerity packages aimed at shoring up the economy. The most radical of these was the International Monetary Fund (IMF) and World Bank-inspired Structural Adjustment Programme (SAP) adopted by the Babangida military government in 1986. Structural adjustment, as has been argued by many Nigerian scholars, fed into the dynamics of economic decline and social-institutional decay that was already under way in the country. The 1980s in Nigeria witnessed several rounds of massive public and private sector retrenchments and redundancies, the drastic erosion of the standard of living of the majority of the people, spiralling inflation and the elimination of subsidies, the imposition of levies for health and educational services, and the collapse of individual and household incomes. The adverse effect of SAP on people's lives and the social unrest it generated (riots in major urban centres, strikes by university teachers, students, doctors, labour unions, and so on) were handled in repressive and high-handed ways by succeeding governments. The rapid deterioration of the national economy and the social decay that resulted reinforced the structures of political repression and authoritarianism. With the state abdicating its social responsibilities and the economy sliding deeper into decline even as political repression and corruption blossomed, the basis for the legitimacy of the post-colonial government was gradually eroded.

Particularly targeted for repression were the associations of Nigerian professionals, workers and the youth whose activism had been central to the construction of a secular, territorial national identity and the containment of the boundaries of political authoritarianism. Most notable among these associations were the Academic Staff Union of Universities, the National Association of Nigerian Students, the Nigerian Medical Association, the National Association of Resident Doctors and the Nigeria Labour Congress and its 42 affiliate unions, among many others. Members of these associations were also activists in various groups like the Movement for a Progressive Nigeria, Youth Solidarity for Southern Africa, the Socialist Congress of Nigeria, and other such formations. The collapse of the national economy in the early 1980s and the crisis management approaches adopted by the state not only took a heavy toll on the membership of these associations through retrenchments and redundancies, but also resulted in the collapse of incomes and opportunities. Furthermore, as they were in the vanguard of the resistance against austerity, including SAP, the groups were also at the receiving end of the most repressive political strategies of the state. It was commonplace in Nigeria in the second half of the 1980s to refer to the collapse of the middle class, as it was once known. As a consequence of this, Nigeria witnessed a realignment of social forces in a manner that produced the three trends referred to earlier, and that reflected a tension between the forces of secularism and parochialism, democracy and authoritarianism, and centralism and decentralisation.

Religious revivalist movements

Both Christian and Islamic religious revivalist movements, including those that are popularly referred to as 'fundamentalists', began to enter into the national consciousness from the mid-1970s (Ibrahim 1989). Their emergence signified a new development in religious practices in the country, as their stated aim was to revive and 'purify' both religions by returning to the 'original' theological sources on which they were supposedly founded. In defining their agenda, both strands of the nascent religious revivalist movements were as sectarian and doctrinaire as they were intolerant of each other and of the practitioners of traditional African religions. Yet the assumption that is often made that the groups are monolithic or homogeneous is an untenable one as, even within each sect, there have always existed differences based on their competing interpretations and usage of religious doctrines as well as on the strategies that they thought were most suitable for the achievement of their objective of religious purification and revival.

In general, two broad strands dominate the global Islamic movement, namely, the 'moderates' and the 'radicals'. Within each of these two strands are groups whose doctrines straddle both the 'moderate' and 'radical' divide. The 'moderates' can be characterised as those who are generally accommodating of the government in power while the 'radicals', on the other hand, are usually critical of and confrontational towards the government and, indeed, all secular authority. They oppose the existing system of politics and governance and view the government's authority as illegitimate, arguing that it is corrupt and un-Islamic. According to Azzam, using the Egyptian example, what differentiates these two groups is the basic belief of the radicals in

> *hakimiyya l'allah*, meaning that sovereignty lies only with God, and *Jihad*, which is described as the missing pillar (*al-farida al-gha'iba*) in Muslim devotional practice. Muslims are called upon to pursue jihad against a ruler deemed to be an un-believer (*kafir*) either by virtue of his not implementing the sharia or corruption (*fasad*) or making peace with the Jews. (Azzam 1996: 111)

In spite of these differences both groups believe that 'Islam is the solution' and the implementation of the Sharia is the answer.

Although the categorisations used in describing the broad trends in the Islamic movement can also be used in classifying their Christian fundamentalist or 'born again' counterparts, I have opted instead to use those categories adopted by Marshall (1993) in her study of the Nigerian Christian (fundamentalist) movement. According to Marshall, the movement is made up of two broad streams, namely those whom she describes as the 'pentecostals' (who are the moderates) and the 'holiness' or 'righteousness' churches (whose members are the radicals) (Marshall 1993: 22). The 'holiness' groups, according to Marshall are 'highly organised and strongly denominational, and [promote] a doctrine which [stresses] strict personal ethics, a retreat from the 'world' and worldly possessions and practices, as well as the imminent second coming of Christ' (ibid.: 22).

In contrast, the ideological belief of the moderates is based on a 'doctrine of prosperity' 'in which the spiritual and material fortunes of a believer were dependent upon whether they gave spiritually and materially to God (or his representatives) who would reward them by 'prospering' them' (ibid.: 22). In addition, their doctrine emphasises experiential faith, the centrality of the Holy Spirit and the spiritual gift of 'speaking in tongues', faith healing and miracles associated with the Pentecost. (ibid.: 22). Although they also stress strict ethical codes and the second coming of Christ, they are not as doctrinaire as their 'holiness' brothers.

Despite these ideological differences, both groups have some points of convergence. The first is their strong opposition to orthodox denominations. The second is that they are instinctively hostile to any Christian church that incorporates traditional African beliefs in its teachings and practices. The third is their total disdain for the followers of African traditional religion as well as for Muslims. Finally, all 'born again' groups have a strict moral code which embodies the following: 'that true believers do not lie, cheat, steal, quarrel, gossip, give or take bribes, drink alcohol, smoke, fornicate, beat their spouses, lose their temper, or deny assistance to other members in need. Strict marital fidelity is a central tenet and divorce is not sanctioned' (ibid.: 23–4).

One major difference between the fundamentalist factions of both religions is their attitude towards politics. Unlike their Muslim counterparts, who see their struggle as political, the Christian fundamentalists have, until recently at least, been mainly apolitical. The change in attitude which has started to take place recently can be attributed to religious clashes during the 1980s between Muslims and Christians in some parts of northern Nigerian (see Ibrahim 1989 and 1991 for details). Consequently, the Christian fundamentalists, through the Pentecostal Fellowship of Nigeria (PFN), adopted an overtly political approach to issues in which they defined Muslims as their political enemies. As Marshall remarks in her observation on this shift: 'frequent references were made to "bad politicians" and the "Islamization" of Nigeria through the make up of Babangida's ruling council, incorporation into the Organisation of Islamic Conference, denial of land for church building, and northern religious "fanaticism"' (Marshall 1993: 35).

Nigerian Islamists

If the global Islamist movement is characterised by the two broad currents described earlier, the Nigerian Islamist movement is made up of three main streams of thoughts. The first is what Imam (1993a: 132) refers to as the 'Political Islamist' stream. This group represents the interests of the Muslim elite in the Jama'atu Nasril Islam (JNI) and the Supreme Council of Islamic Affairs (SCIA). It is made up of members of the political establishment. The objective of this strand is the political control of the state and its apparatuses, but not for the purpose, strictly speaking, of imposing radical Islamic reforms.

In seeking to maintain their political influence, members of this stream often resort to whipping up sentiments with a view to portraying themselves as 'good' Muslims and thus winning support for themselves among the members of the more radical, fundamentalist stream. This can be observed from the role of its members in the 1978 and 1988 Constituent Assembly debates over the application of Sharia. As Imam noted, 'the need for mass support' led this group into embracing fundamentalist positions on certain issues: 'the agitation for a Federal

Sharia Court of Appeal equally ranked with the Federal Court of Appeal has been increasingly argued, not simply as for those who wish to apply it, but for the "Muslim communities of Nigeria"' (ibid.: 132–3). But once in power, the representatives of this stream have often acted to repress challenges from the fundamentalist factions to their authority and the secular basis of the Nigerian state. They are often targeted for this reason by the fundamentalists as corrupt and treacherous. It is under the aegis of this group that FOMWAN, our case study organisation, was established.

The second strand is the moderate one represented by the Jamaat Izalat Al-Bidi'awa Iqamat Al Sunna, commonly known as Izala, and its members, the Yan Izala. This group was founded in the late 1970s by Ismail Idris, a soldier who served in the Nigerian army as an Imam (Kukah 1993: 217). However, the group became synonymous with its grand patron, the late Alhaji Abubakar Gumi, Nigeria's Ambassador to Saudi Arabia in the 1950s, Grand Qhadi of the defunct northern Nigeria (1963–1967), recipient of the King Faizal International Award for service to Islam (1987), Chairman of the Islamic Pilgrims Board (1975) and Grand Mufti (the Grand Jurisconsult of Islamic law) of Nigeria in 1976. The emergence of this group, according to Kukah, 'was the climax of years of Alhaji Gumi's search for a political platform based on his religious beliefs and the search for an independent political and economic base for himself' (Kukah 1993: 218). The raison d'être of this group is

> based upon a puritanical, 'return to the source' approach aimed to save Islam from syncretist and thus un-Islamic practices. This return to source operates at two levels. First, it involves a frontal attack against remnants of traditional African religious practices still prevalent among Muslim communities. Secondly, it involves a struggle against mystical practices and the beliefs of sufi brotherhoods (Darika), mainly the Tijaniyya and Quadiriyya. (Ibrahim 1989: 71)

Thus, it sees its role as partially entailing the re-conversion of the members of the sufi brotherhoods who it believes have been led astray. Other characteristics of this group include its disapproval of ostentatious naming ceremonies, exorbitant marriage payments, the act of prostrating before anybody as all men (sic) are equal, celebration of the Prophet's birthday, correct rituals for prayer and fasting, abstention from drugs including alcohol and cigarettes, 'proper' behaviour by women and the discouragement of its members from praying in mosques not managed by its own Imams or those with similar beliefs (Imam 1993a: 132, Kukah 1993: 218). As the group is patronised by the Saudi authorities, it echoes its master's voice by being anti-Ahmadiyya, pro-business, and anti-sufi.

Since the Yan Izala is opposed to the brotherhoods whose members dominate the Muslim establishment, it seeks to recruit its followers from among the growing array of the urban and social poor in Nigeria. This is not to suggest that the top leadership of the group lacks influence or has no political clout. Far from it. But the majority of its members have been drawn from among the destitute urban poor, including the poorest echelons of the working class, the army of déclassé or lumpen elements, and new and ill-adapted migrants in urban centres from rural areas. These are social categories whose ranks swelled during the 1980s and the 1990s as the Nigerian economic crisis took its toll (Ibrahim 1989, Imam 1993a). As part of its membership drive, the Izala organises regular campaigns in the north of Nigeria and also sells recorded cassettes.

Women account for a significant proportion of the Izala Movement's membership. Regular religious classes are organised for them. In fact, the organisation's women's programme was incorporated into that of the Centre for Adult Education, which is affiliated to the Ahmadu Bello University, Zaria (Ibrahim 1989). Despite this, Alhaji Gumi had an essentially negative perspective on women's roles in the public domain. Although he urged women to play a positive role in the politics of the aborted Third Republic, he viewed leadership roles as an exclusively male affair. He noted that 'women can be very useful' in some aspects of politics, but 'to make them mix [with men] like Europeans is not acceptable to Islam' (interview quoted in Birai 1993: 196). In continuation of his offensive against women, Alhaji Gumi had categorically stated that it was his hope not to see a woman leading Nigeria while he was still alive.

In contrast to the political Islamists and moderates, the radical strand in the Nigerian Islamist movement rejects the idea of a secular state and constitution and considers the Iranian model of governance as being ideal for Nigeria. Organisations within this strand have close links with the Iranian government and depend on it for both material and financial support. Their basic tenet is that a Jihad should be waged by all Muslims until the Sharia becomes national law, and that the battle for an Islamic state in Nigeria should start with the destruction of the secular state (ibid.: 197). The most prominent members of this group are drawn from Mallam Ibrahim El Zakzaky's Islamic Movement (which is based in Zaria) and the Council of Ulama. Both groups metamorphosed from the Muslim Student Society (MSS). El Zakzaky, the leader of the Islamic Movement, was expelled from the Ahmadu Bello University during the 1978 student crisis and has had frequent clashes with the security forces since then (Ibrahim 1989). As for the Council of Ulama, it signifies, as Kukah puts it, the 'coming of age, the adulthood of the MSS' (Kukah 1993: 221) from university campuses into mainstream religious discourses. The organisation attributed its founding in part to the 'growing influence of Zionism as the Federal Government continues to lean more heavily on Israeli security cover, [which] means that hard days lie ahead for Islam' (ibid.: 221).

The MSS was founded in 1954 as an organisation of Yoruba Muslim students (Ibrahim 1989: 73). It developed, however, into a national organisation with branches in most schools and institutions of higher learning. Its objectives at inception were the organisation of prayers, fellowship and evangelism among students. However, since the mid-1970s a hard core extremist group has ascended to and retained the leadership of the organisation both at the national level and in the centres of Islamic radicalism in the universities of Zaria, Kano and Sokoto (ibid.: 73). The organisation gained national prominence between 1976 and 1977 during the Constitution Drafting Committee (CDC) and Constituent Assembly debates on Sharia. The MSS stated that 'we stand for total application of the Sharia, both as a legal system and a way of life. The Sharia is not reducible, nor can it be compartmentalised. Therefore, the Muslims would require nothing less than a total application of the Sharia and its full entrenchment in the constitution' (Ibrahim Yacub quoted in Ibrahim 1989: 73). The radical Islamists, like their moderate and political counterparts, can boast of a sizeable female membership. The Muslim Sisters Organisation (MSO) is the women's wing of this group.

While the political Islamists have a different view on the role and place of Muslim women in society, the moderates and the radicals, despite their differences over the tactics and strategies for achieving their objectives, espouse the same gender ideology. According to Imam,

these groups are broadly in agreement that women, although having equal souls before Allah, are under the jurisdiction of men as fathers and husbands on earth. These groups also see women as having a different physiology to men, which fits them essentially for the role of mother and wife. In this role, however, the fundamentalists stress the physical seclusion of women, while the political Islamists are more willing to concede that women may venture out of the home, if only they will dress decently and avoid unnecessary interactions with men. Furthermore, the fundamentalists support education of women primarily in order to enable them to be better teachers to their children and to be able to proselytise among women. The political Islamists accept this objective but also see roles for women in the wider economy — mostly in sex-stereotyped jobs. Fundamentalists defend the right of men to marry barely pubertal girls, political Islamists often advise waiting a little. (Imam 1993a: 133)

Nigerian Christian religious groups

The origins of the 'holiness' or radical Christian groups can be traced back to the activities of British and American missionaries between the 1920s and 1950s. Among the earliest churches to be established within this ideological strand were the Faith Tabernacle, the Apostolic Church, the Apostolic Faith and the Assemblies of God (Marshall 1993: 22). Indigenous brands of these churches such as the Redeemed Christian Church of God and the Deeper Life Bible Church were later established as part of the 'holiness' order. Membership was drawn mostly from the literate and semi-literate indigent group. To back up its strict moral doctrine, a strict dress code was established for the female membership, members were forbidden to watch television and adorn themselves with jewellery. In addition to the spiritual and moral guidance they provide, these churches have established a social support system to provide succour to members in times of need.

The 'pentecostals' or moderates emerged on the Nigerian religious landscape in the 1970s and 1980s from their bases in the universities. Unlike their 'holiness' brethren, this brand of the Christian religious movement, which grew out of the academy, was made up of young and highly educated individuals who placed a high premium on material success. It is therefore not surprising that the pentecostals treasure the same symbols of status and prestige (fine clothes, smart cars, foreign goods, and so on) which most non-fundamentalists in the wider society fancy.

There is very little difference in the views of the 'holiness' and 'pentecostals' streams of the new Christian movement on the gender roles of women and men. Apart from the 'holiness' churches' strict moral and dress code for women, their confinement of women to lower levels of church administration and their endorsement of most of the popular stereotypes of non-'born again' women as 'temptresses', 'witches', 'spendthrifts' or 'nymphomaniacs', both streams of thought support the spiritual doctrines on the 'submission of women to men and their confinement to the domestic sphere' (ibid.: 29). At the same time, husbands are called upon to treat their wives with respect and consideration by involving them in family decisions, participating in domestic chores, and playing a role in child rearing and caring activities. Despite sanctioning women's subordinate status in relation to their husbands, there is still a sense in which the fundamentalist doctrines that the churches preach could be said at one level to be a partially 'liberating' force in the lives of their female members in the areas of marriage, sexuality and family life. Infidelity, divorce and violence against women, which are rampant in the wider society and which men think are their legitimate rights, are frowned upon and condemned by the Christian fundamentalists. In addition, these churches advocate the use of contraceptives to regulate women's fertility.

At another level, however, the doctrinal injunction which they emphasise for women to obey their husbands reproduces patriarchal structures in a social context where obedience is taken to mean total submission by the woman to the man, including submission to his arbitrary whims and caprices. It is therefore not too surprising that even when their husbands are more faithful and eschew violence, Christian women members of the fundamentalist churches are unable to translate this into a wider struggle for advocating their rights as women because the gains offered to them from membership of the church are a function of their acceptance of a subordinate position to their husbands in the household. In this sense, the 'liberating' effect of the message of the new Christian movement is a highly partial one which is contingent on the willingness of the male members of the church to run a 'responsible' household and lead a 'responsible' life. It is a partial 'liberation' which emerges by default and which collapses should the man change his commitment to the church.

The Nigerian women's movement

Before the 1980s, the Nigerian women's movement was dominated by the existence of one umbrella national women's organisation, the National Council of Women's Societies (NCWS), and a host of grassroots, village and community-level groupings. However, this situation changed radically in the 1980s with the emergence of Women in Nigeria (WIN) in 1983, the Federation of Muslim Women's Associations in Nigeria (FOMWAN) in 1985, the establishment of the state-funded Better Life Programme for Rural Women (BLP) in 1987, and the growth of a host of national grassroots community development associations as well as several groups working on women's rights issues.

The NCWS, the government-recognised umbrella organisation for women, was created out of the struggle between radical, anti-establishment women and conservative, pro-government women for pre-eminence in and the dominance over the female space. With active government support, the conservative faction won the leadership battle. The NCWS was thus established in 1959 as a non-political and non-religious organisation devoted to the promotion of the education, welfare and improved status of Nigerian women (see Mba 1982 for details). In recent years, however, the organisation has broadened its focus to include women's legal and political rights by promoting political awareness campaigns during elections and demanding a change in some of the laws that dehumanise womanhood (Abdullah 1994).

Although the NCWS sees itself as an advocate for women's rights in Nigeria, the organisation's gender ideology, rather than liberating women, reinforces patriarchy. In demanding the recognition of women's rights, the NCWS has always been quick to point out that it is only seeking 'complementary roles for women rather than competitive roles such that when demands are made by women, they are punctuated by assurances that they do not constitute a confrontation with the male establishment or challenge to traditional family patterns' (Kisekka 1992: 116). Additionally, some of the NCWS viewpoints have been detrimental to the advancement of Nigerian women's interests. For example, the organisation lobbied politicians against the 1981 Abortion Bill to legalise abortion and has persistently urged poor Nigerians, especially women, to tighten their belts and endure the harsh economic policies of various governments since 1981 when the Nigerian economy went into crisis (Imam 1993a, Abdullah 1994).

In contrast to the NCWS, Women in Nigeria (WIN), Nigeria's first feminist organisation, takes a radical and critical stance on the issue of gender inequalities in society. On the issue of gender subordination in Nigeria, WIN states that 'The majority of women, like the majority of men, suffer from the exploitative and oppressive character of the Nigerian society; women suffer additional forms of exploitation and oppression; women therefore suffer double oppression and exploitation as members of subordinate classes and as women' (WIN 1985). The organisation states further that 'the liberation of women cannot be fully achieved outside the context of the oppressed and poor majority of the people'.

In pursuit of its objective of 'transforming gender relations to achieve gender equality in society', WIN has forged alliances with other popular democratic forces in the country (Abdullah 1995, Imam 1993b, Shettima 1991). The organisation's activities are mainly in the areas of research and documentation, dissemination of information, advocacy, political conscientisation and project work. The rallying slogan of the organisation centres on the notion that 'every issue is a women's issue ... [and] every women's issue is everyone's concern' (Imam 1993b). It is on the basis of this that the organisation has campaigned against child marriages, purdah, sexual harassment and violence against women. Additionally, WIN has included issues of women's reproductive rights and choice, sexual harassment and violence, and consciousness-raising programmes in its broader discourse on and action programme for Nigerian women (Abdullah 1994, 1995).

The Federation of Muslim Women's Associations in Nigeria (FOMWAN) was founded in 1985, with the objective of liberating Muslims within the parameters of Islamic law. A detailed discussion of the organisation will be undertaken later in this essay and so I will not go into a detailed description of its work here.

In 1987 a new trend emerged within the Nigerian women's movement. This trend has had far-reaching consequences both within and outside of the movement. The new trend centred on the launch of the Better Life Programme for Rural Women (BLP) by the government of General Ibrahim Babangida (1985–93). The establishment of this programme ushered in a new era in the development of women's groups in Nigeria, as it heralded the twin processes of state feminism and 'wifeism'. The former refers to the process of direct intervention by the state in the formation and funding of a women's 'development' programme, while the latter refers to the appointment of wives of high-ranking government officials as leaders of the organisation set up as part of the project of state feminism (Abdullah 1994).

The BLP's objective, according to its former National Co-ordinator, Mrs Maryam Babangida, was to create a 'new rural woman' – economically strong, politically active, socially aware, psychologically fulfilled, and thus equipped to play her role in society to the fullest (Babangida 1991). To achieve these objectives, the BLP organised literacy and vocational training courses, social welfare and health programmes, enlightenment campaigns and income-generating projects for women. But the administrative structure of the project and its ideological orientation supported gender subordination in the society, by mirroring and reproducing the state's conservative image of women as wives, mothers and secondary income earners. Furthermore, the automatic appointment of wives based on their husbands' status in the state political and military hierarchy, regardless of their suitability or merit, not only was undemocratic but also reinforced the prevailing societal image of women as appendages to male power (Abdullah 1995).

To further the policy of state feminism and wifeism, a National Commission for Women (NCW) was established in 1989, with the wife of the president as a life member of the board of the Commission. A National Centre for Women's Development was built and named after the wife of the president. However, after General Babangida was forced out of office in August 1993, the BLP and all that went with it became history. The wife of the new head of state, Mrs Mariam Abacha, launched her own programme, the Family Support Programme (FSP), changed the name of the National Centre and had the NCW upgraded to a ministry. Even though some of these changes were welcomed by critics of the former regime (such as the change of name of the centre and the upgrading of the NCW), the ideological orientation of the regime on women's issues did not change. If anything, things became worse as the Abacha junta unleashed an unprecedented reign of terror against the generality of Nigerians. FSP itself has become the focal point for a personality cult around Mrs Abacha, while the ministry is subject to her arbitrary whims and authoritarian style. Both the BLP and the FSP also pose serious constitutional and governance issues.

The human rights and civil liberties movement

Perhaps more than the two social movements discussed in the preceding sections, the Nigerian human rights and civil liberties movement was entirely an outgrowth of the socio-economic and political conditions prevailing in the country in the 1980s. In order to understand the origins and growth of this movement, a brief outline of the factors that triggered its emergence in the Nigerian landscape is worth repeating. In this regard, it should be noted that the return of the military, with their disregard for basic civil liberties and human rights at a time of national economic decline and socio-political disquiet, was a factor in the development of the civil rights movement. In their attempt to solve the economic and political problems of the country, the military regime of Generals Buhari and Idiagbon (1983–5) moved against a variety of interest groups throughout the country. Politicians and political activities were banned, several professional and student organisations were proscribed, journalists, activists and politicians were arrested and detained, and decrees were promulgated to limit the press and prevent public discussions of the country's political future, particularly the prospective date for the return to civil rule (Olukoshi 1994: 2). This atmosphere of terror and repression was carried forward by the Babangida administration (1985–93) and continued, with greater intensity than before, under the regime of General Abacha (1993–8).

Given the tense and repressive political atmosphere in the country, as well as the dwindling economic fortunes of most Nigerians, it did not come as a surprise when, in 1987, the Civil Liberties Organisation (CLO) was launched as Nigeria's premier human rights organisation. Although the Nigerian human and civil rights movement is made up of over thirty groupings scattered across the country, two organisations are particularly important for my discussion here. These are the Legal Research and Resource Development Centre (LRRDC) and the International Federation of Women Lawyers (FIDA).

The LRRDC is the first human rights NGO in Nigeria to be founded by a woman. The organisation was established in 1990 by Tokunbo Ige, a lawyer. Its objectives are the provision of human rights education and legal services to the poor and the protection and, where possible, the enforcement of their rights. LRRDC's work is mainly among illiterate, poor and marginalised groups in the society. In this regard, because women make up the majority of the poor and illiterate, women's issues constitute the bulk of the organisation's work, as can be seen from its action programmes and its publications. These programmes and publications cover such issues as the custody of children, divorce and separation, maintenance, marriage, rape, and women and the right of residency. Additionally, the organisation provides legal aid services to women and trains female paralegals. Despite its pro-women programme bias, the organisation sees itself primarily as a human rights organisation and not a women's human rights NGO.

FIDA Nigeria is an affiliate of the International Federation of Women Lawyers. It is an international women's human rights NGO which was established in Nigeria in 1964. The organisation's main project is the provision of free legal service to indigent women and children. Most of the caseloads in FIDA's files relate to custody, abuse and other domestic issues. Although FIDA's focus is on women's human rights, its gender discourse does not threaten the status quo. According to an executive member of the organisation,

> When African women demand equality, we are only asking for our rights not to be tampered with, and the removal of laws that oppress and dehumanise women. We are not asking for equality with our husbands. We accept them as the bosses and heads of the family. (Interview with Obiageli Nwankwo quoted in Abdullah 1995)

The Federation of Muslim Women's Association in Nigeria (FOMWAN)

In the preceding section, I focused on the emergence and character of three types of associational groups that have dominated the Nigerian political landscape during the 1980s and 1990s. In this section, I will focus attention on the Federation of Muslim Women's Association in Nigeria, the first national women's religious organisation to be established in the country and which is dedicated to promoting the rights of Muslim women in the country within the framework of Islam. My critique of FOMWAN's experience attempts to show both the possibilities offered by an approach to advancing women's rights that uses the idiom of religion, and the limitations of this approach as set by the doctrinal foundations and practice of religion itself.

I have earlier pointed out that FOMWAN (or the Federation) was founded in 1985. The organisation sees itself first and foremost as a Muslim women's religious organisation devoted to providing religious education for its members. However, the organisation justifies its existence on the grounds of the non-implementation or non-recognition by the Nigerian Islamic establishment of Muslim women's rights as stated in the Sharia (for example, their right to education, to inheritance, to custody of children at divorce, and a woman's right to divorce if the husband is cruel or impotent, among others), and the prevalence of other un-Islamic practices that violate these rights.

Zainab Kabir, one of the intellectuals of FOMWAN, stated that it is culture or tradition, rather than religion, that is responsible for the subordination of Muslim women. Using seclusion as an example, Kabir notes that Islam does not sanction the seclusion of women in the home, but the avoidance of immoral behaviour and indecent dress (Kabir 1985). She thus advocates women's participation in the 'public' domain provided that they dress modestly. She notes further that most of the citations used to justify women's subordinate position are based on *hadith* and Sharia (which are interpretations of learned scholars), and not on *suras* (Quranic verses). As such, these interpretations must be contextualised within the specific historical framework in which they were made. She also points out that most of the practitioners of *tasfir* (exegesis) were men who interpreted the *suras* and *hadith* without any consideration for women's interests. As a result, she urges women to become scholars and make their own interpretations.

It is within the context of the contestations over doctrinal interpretation that FOMWAN has attempted to define a role for itself. It can thus be said that the organisation was founded with the aim of putting Muslim women's concerns squarely on the national women's agenda. According to a leading FOMWAN activist, the organisation was formed 'to address problems affecting Muslim women such as their education and rights under the Sharia which can only be satisfactorily dealt with by Muslim women, in co-operation with their male counterparts. Because the problems of a Muslim community can only be cured by Islamic solutions' (Yusuf 1991: 99).

The organisation's aims and objectives, as outlined in its constitution, are to promote the education and social development of Muslim women; to encourage and propagate Islam; to advance the recognition of Muslim women's right under the Sharia; to promote unity and co-operation among Muslim women's organisations; and to empower Muslim women to exercise a positive influence on national matters with a view to safeguarding the interests of Islam (ibid.: 100)

Yet quite ironically, FOMWAN officials, in articulating their goals, have, like the NCWS, also been keen to emphasise that their aim is not to strive for equality between men and women. As Lateefat Okunnu, a former president of FOMWAN, observed, the federation does not encourage women to demand equality with men because God has created women and men differently and has thus assigned them different roles in society (interview with Okunnu quoted in Abdullah 1994). Thus, even as it strives to employ Islam as an instrument in its struggle for the advancement of the rights of Muslim women, FOMWAN's outlook on gender also tends to reinforce existing gender inequalities in a society where the structures of patriarchy are very strong. The contradiction between FOMWAN's attempt to use religion to promote reform in favour of women's rights and its refusal to embrace the notion of gender equality perhaps explains why the organisation's action programmes have been generally low-key.

The politics of FOMWAN

In discussing the actions the federation has taken to achieve its aims and objectives, I shall also look at the factors which have hindered or facilitated that process. In furtherance of its objectives, FOMWAN has established schools to educate Muslim women about their rights as stated in the Sharia. It has also campaigned against practices such as the *talaq* (the unilateral divorce by husbands), and forced and early marriages, which violate the rights of Muslim women in Nigeria. Furthermore, FOMWAN has actively engaged in *da'wah* (welfare activities), charity works, and income-generating projects for Muslim women.

But why is it that, despite its twelve years of existence, its close affinity with the Muslim establishment and the state, and the magnitude of the task that exists in the niche it has carved for itself, FOMWAN has not initiated or demanded any significant changes in the conduct of family and marriage relations for the benefit of those for whom it claims to speak? Apart from the contradiction that expressed itself in FOMWAN's desire to employ the medium of Islam to advance women's rights without fighting for gender equality, the federation has not been willing or able to press for far-reaching legal reforms to change existing gender relations with a view to improving the lives of women within its professed constituency, because its formation was primarily a political project aimed at countering NCWS and managing change, rather than of promoting a radical transformatory project (Abdullah 1996). Furthermore, the ideological orientation of its leadership is one that encourages the subordination of women to men. In relation to the latter, rather than engage the state and its allies in its struggle for women's rights, FOMWAN has busied itself more with criticising and picking holes in every proposal on Nigerian women made by the NCWS, the organisation with which it competes for state largesse.

For example, the proposal put forward by the NCWS to protect the rights of women in marriage (to check the increasing rate of divorce and to protect women's rights on divorce, as most Nigerian women are divorced without alimony or any form of benefit) was subjected to criticism by FOMWAN. In its proposal, NCWS wanted the government to make it mandatory for any man who wishes to terminate a marriage that has lasted for ten years or more to relinquish half of his assets to the wife he intends to divorce (Yusuf 1991: 99). FOMWAN felt the proposal was biased against Muslim women who were in polygamous marriages and that it was un-Islamic, as it failed to recognise the Islamic law of inheritance.

Most offensive to Muslim women was the assumption that a man had only one wife: the proposal did not allow for the situation of his having up to four wives, most of whom had lived with him for ten or more years. If half a Muslim man's assets were awarded to one divorced wife (assuming she would ever receive the amount), it would result in adverse effects for the children and wives who remained in the family. (ibid.: 100)

Although the proposal failed to take cognisance of the situation of Muslim women and women married under customary law who may be in polygamous relations, and although it also displayed ignorance of the Islamic law of inheritance, rather than engage in a negative war of attrition in the press FOMWAN could have requested a meeting with the NCWS leadership to iron out their differences. Instead, as part of its campaign against the proposal, FOMWAN labelled NCWS a Zionist organisation because of its alleged domination by Christians (*New Nigerian*, 15 July 1989).

Secondly, it is impossible for FOMWAN to campaign for legal reforms to give Muslim women a more equal status with men because this would violate its self-appointed mandate and lead to the ultimate loss of support and favour it presently enjoys from the influential Muslim establishment and the state at the local and national levels. Since the women in the FOMWAN leadership are not willing to forgo these benefits (and the lifestyles that are built on them), they have been extremely reluctant to push for changes that will transform the lives of Nigerian Muslim women.

Religion, human rights and and the struggle for women's rights in Nigeria

From the discussion so far, it can be deduced that neither the human rights groups nor the women's religious groups and the 'state feminists' have concerned themselves sufficiently with the issues of the state and family in their struggles for women's rights. Several reasons account for the neglect of these two institutions as sites for the contestation of women's human rights in Nigeria. Firstly, there is the perception of all these social movement groups (with the exception of WIN) of their roles in society as non-political. Flowing from this self-perception is the implication that they cannot confront the state with demands to improve or transform gender relations in society. Although WIN is an exception in this regard, as it explicitly defines its mission as political, it must also be noted that the organisation has not been able to infuse its progressive gender ideology into the discourses or struggles of its allies in the human rights movement (Abdullah 1994). The Christian women, apart from being non-political, are not a unified group dedicated to the promotion of women's rights within the church. Rather, the sermons and doctrines about family and matrimonial life to which they are exposed are designed to prepare them to be good wives.

The second reason why the various groups have not sufficiently concerned themselves with reform of the state and family laws centres on the fact that many of the leading organisations like FOMWAN and NCWS owe their creation and continued existence to the state and its allies. This being the case, it is inconceivable that they will make demands on the state for radical social transformation.

The family has not featured significantly in the struggle for women's rights in Nigeria for much the same reason as in countries like Lebanon where, as Joseph observes,

[the] family ... has been pivotal for social, economic, and political existence and well-being. This has been so across social classes, regions and religious/ethnic groups. It is, therefore, not accidental that human rights movements in the Middle East have not fully addressed the family. ... While there is increasing recognition that the family is not immune to human rights issues, women's movements in the Middle East have been careful to differentiate their concerns about family from those of Western feminists whom they often perceive as having been at times anti-family. (Joseph 1993: 148)

In addition to the above, the artificial dichotomisation of society into the 'private' and 'public' realms has contributed to the near neglect of the family as a site for the struggle for women's human rights in Nigeria. Whereas issues relating to women's role in the productive sector and outside the home are discussed in the public sphere, those regarding the status of women within the family and their reproductive roles and functions are addressed in the private realm, where the state and the many civil society-based organisations have adopted the precepts of 'respect for privacy and non-interference by the state'.

Yet, in ignoring the state and the family as sites for the contestation of women's rights, the various groups that dominate the religious, human rights and women's movements have failed in their quest to promote women's human rights in Nigeria. These two institutions are important in the discussion on women's rights because of their pivotal roles in the construction of rights in society. The state is important as a location for the contestation of women's human rights because of its role in either promoting or discouraging these rights. As to the family, its role in the protection or disregard of women's human rights is significant because the family in Nigeria, as in most African societies, is the focal social institution for primary social interaction. It provides its members with various social identities with which they come to associate themselves later in life.

Within the broad framework of its essentially patriarchal foundation, the attitude exhibited by the Nigerian state towards women varies from time to time according to whether the incumbent regime is more or less conservative than its predecessor. During the Second Republic (1979–83), the overwhelmingly establishment National Party of Nigeria (NPN), the ruling party, was supportive of the conservative views of the NCWS on women's issues. The actions of the austere Buhari–Idiagbon military administration (31 December 1983–27 August 1985), which took power in a coup d'état, was based on the ruling junta's conception of the causes of the Nigerian economic and political crises, a conception which had implications for its attitude towards women. According to the junta, the crisis was a result of the corruption and indiscipline of the civilian population. Hence, the regime embarked on a campaign to wipe out these twin 'evils'. Women were targeted in this campaign under the rubric of the War Against Indiscipline (WAI) programme. They were scapegoated and accused of ruining the economy by profiteering. This led to many women being arrested and having their enterprises destroyed. Women were also implicitly held responsible for the pervading corruption and delinquency in the Second Republic. It was often suggested that men became corrupt in order to satisfy the material demands of women. Consequently, women were admonished to be good wives, citizens and mothers, through radio and television jingles. Single women were arrested in several parts of the country and forced to get married. Informal sector women, including commercial sex workers, were generally harassed by state security forces (Dennis 1987).

Although the Babangida regime, which took power in a palace coup and ruled for nine years (27 August 1985–27 August 1993) until it was forced out of power, was just as repressive as its predecessor, it took an apparently liberal attitude towards women and women's issues by establishing and funding a state women's programme run by General Babangida's wife and those of his colleagues in the military junta and political bureaucracy. As has been argued elsewhere (Abdullah 1993, 1994, 1995), the regime's focus on women should be understood within the logic of the SAP that it initiated. Although there was very little difference in substance between the political and economic programmes pursued by the Babangida and Abacha regimes, on the women's question there is a divergence between them. This difference has its roots in the history of petty jealousy and rivalry between the wives of the two men.

During the BLP era, Mrs Abacha, as wife of the then Minister of Defence, Chairman of the Joint Chiefs of Staff and Chief of Army Staff (Abacha held all of these positions at various times) was conspicuously absent from the activities of the programme. She concentrated on her role as the chairperson of the Army Officers' Wives Association, a role she inherited from Mrs Babangida after the latter's husband became the head of state. It was therefore not surprising that when she assumed the role of Nigeria's first lady, she set out to systematically dismantle all structures and programmes that had been established by Mrs Babangida. Thus the BLP was replaced by the FSP. Unlike the BLP, which had women's 'empowerment' within the existing structures of the state and society as its slogan, the FSP's ideology was based on a conservative, traditional conception of the family, with women's roles being defined primarily as those of mothers and wives. As such, the first almanac prepared in 1995 to publicise the programme had the photograph of Mrs Abacha carrying a child on her back!

The family as a provider of economic security and social identities, and as a social institution where members learn the culture and values of their societies in their formative years, defines for its members the initial meaning of the concept of rights as well as rewards and sanctions for different kinds of behaviour. Because of the patriarchal character of the family, male members are favoured over women in the construction of rights and the values on which they rest. This act of privileging males over females feeds directly into the relations of subordination and discrimination that women experience in the wider society.

Expanding the definition of human rights: CEDAW

While pointing out the weaknesses of the various social movements involved in the struggle for women's rights in Nigeria, it must be noted also that their inability to articulate women's rights issues in their entirety stems from the way concepts of rights have been constructed historically. The discourse on rights can be traced to the pre-Enlightenment period when rights were based on 'divine authority' or 'natural' law to be enjoyed only by propertied men. Women (even those from the propertied class) were excluded by the discourse. Not even the changes associated with the liberal democratic revolution brought women into the rights discourse. It is this historical bias against women which informed all discourses on rights until the adoption, in 1948, of the Universal Declaration of Human Rights by the United Nations.

Using the example of the CEDAW, the Women's Convention, this section of the discussion will focus on how the UN, as an important arena for the definition of the international human rights system, has broadened the framework of human rights to include the human rights of women. Although the UN committed itself to gender equality from its inception, it was not until 1979, when CEDAW or the Women's Convention was adopted, that a legal framework for eliminating gender-based discrimination came into being. It thus became the first UN human rights instrument specifically devoted to the advancement of women's human rights, establishing binding norms for state parties and acting as a machinery to put pressure on national authorities. CEDAW focuses on such issues as the elimination of discrimination against women in political participation, nationality, education, employment, health, property, residence, marriage and family. According to Tomasevski, the uniqueness of the Women's Convention lies in the fact that it requires 'state parties to tackle discrimination in the private lives and relationships of their citizens and not simply in public sector activities' (Tomasevski 1993: 115).

Since the Women's Convention came into force in 1981, over half of the UN member nations have ratified it. But why is it that, despite its wide acceptance by the international community and its noble objectives, women's rights are still fiercely contested within human rights theory and practice? Part of the explanation lies in the fact that although the Women's Convention has been ratified by more than half of UN member nations, and accepted by most human rights NGOs as a human rights instrument, it is not legally binding upon them. This is because the Women's Convention has a clause within it allowing states to note their reservations about the Convention, or even opt out of some of its requirements. Latching onto this clause, most signatories entered some reservations which gave them the right to continue applying discriminatory policies against women. Tomasevski noted that 'most reservations have been entered with respect to non-discrimination in family law and citizenship, and to women's legal capacity' (ibid.: 117).

Concerned about the effects the reservations might have on the Women's Convention, the UN Sub-Commission on Prevention of Discrimination and Protection of Minorities noted with grave concern

> that certain reservations to the Convention, in particular those in relation to the adoption of policies and institutional measures to implement the terms of the Convention (art. 2), political and public life (art. 7), discrimination in the field of employment (art. 11), equality of men and women before the law (art. 15) and marriage and family relations (art. 16) might diminish the international legal norm and legitimise its violation. (quoted in Tomasevski 1993: 119)

Other factors limiting the work of the CEDAW's monitoring body include its lack of a mandate to enforce the Convention, to receive complaints from individual women about violations of their rights, and to reject reservations if they are inimical to the overall objectives of the Convention. These obstacles put in the way of CEDAW's monitoring body should not come as a surprise to feminist activists because, despite its commitment to gender equality, the UN, in addition to remaining an essentially male-dominated institution that still, on the whole, visualises women's roles and functions in society from a male perspective, is guided by liberal notions of the division of the world into the 'public' and 'private' realms. This dichotomisation of the world into two separate spheres has relegated discriminatory practices against women to the 'private' domain where they cannot be regulated by international law. How else can one explain the inclusion of a reservation clause in the Women's Convention, whose application could lead to radical transformation in the lives of women?

Concluding remarks

The three currents in associational life in contemporary Nigeria which I have reviewed in this essay depict, from different angles, the difficulty that continues to prevail in the country with regard to the protection and advancement of women's rights. From their different positions, the various associations either showed total disregard for women's rights issues or were incapable of dealing with them. The religious revivalist movement's position represents an essentially right-wing response to the issue of women's roles and functions in society. Apart from systematically ignoring many women's rights issues in their discourses on women, these religious organisations also defend the subordination of women to men in all spheres of society. As to the human rights movement, because its core members work in a purely legalistic and non-political context it has been unable, despite all its potential, to initiate radical programmes that will focus on women's human rights concerns.

Unlike the religious and human rights movements, the women's movement is the most diverse. It has within its ranks a non-religious conservative grouping, a religious conservative organisation, conservative state-funded groups and a feminist organisation. Apart from the feminist group that addresses women's human rights concerns, the others have not done so for the reasons which I adduced. Despite its shortcomings, which have been pointed out, WIN is the most successful organisation within the women's movement in bringing the women's question to the centre of the political discourse in Nigeria, although it has been less successful in getting its political allies in the pro-democracy movement to embrace its main message.

The inability of the human rights and women's movements to infuse women's human rights concerns into their struggle for women's rights is partly also the result of the continuing dominance of the private–public dichotomy in both human rights and women's movements activism. Matters are not helped in this regard by the limitations of the international human rights regime as manifested in the example of CEDAW. In order for the international human rights system to be able to incorporate women's rights issues into a radical transformatory project, a reconceptualisation of human rights concepts is needed. For example, the questioning by certain groups and communities of their exclusion within the existing human rights framework has challenged the assumption of the universality of the concept of human rights. What is needed is a more inclusive and holistic concept of human rights that will embrace the needs and aspirations of all minority and historically marginalised groups, including women.

Some attention needs to be paid to the interface between prolonged economic crisis, exacerbated by structural adjustment, continuing political authoritarianism and the transformation of popular identities, including religious ones, and the ways in which these factors affect women's rights in contemporary Africa. What are the possibilities open to women, the constraints continuing to face them and the obstacles they have to confront in the context of the underlying changes taking place in African economies, politics and society? This is a critical question which has to be carefully addressed if the struggle for the advancement of the rights and interests of women is to be relevant and meaningful to them. In this regard, the various groups, especially the non-religious ones in the vanguard of the rights struggle in Nigeria, need to make gender as a category more central to their analysis because, as an analytical concept, it has the same status as class, ethnicity, race, the state and the world system, dealing as it does with the structural relationship between men and women and linked as it is to the state, economy and micro- and macro-processes and institutions (Moghadam 1990: 8).

Few will disagree that in Nigeria today, women's rights and concerns continue to be trampled upon in spite of the apparent interest from above, at the level of the state, in women's affairs. The challenge which this poses to the non-state groups concerned with the promotion of the welfare and rights of women is for them to seek ways of working together on a common, minimum programme for the promotion of the rights of Nigerian women. For all the differences among the non-state groups – and these are many – and for the social, organisational and political contexts within which they work, it is still possible to identify a number of action programmes on which the various groups can agree, including areas of legal, political and constitutional reform that will have direct bearing on women's roles in the family and polity. As a first step towards the forging of a minimum action programme on which all or most of the non-state groups can agree, and which could serve as their campaigning points over the specified period of time, it is proposed that they convene an all-Nigeria summit on women that brings together the women's, human rights and religious groups interested in the women's question, to develop and adopt such an action programme. Such a summit, if it is to be successful, will necessarily involve a spirit of give and take on the part of all the groups and strands relevant to the struggles of Nigerian women.

Chapter Six

Tensions in legal and religious values in the 1996 South African Constitution

Ebrahim Moosa

Law and religion

It is no longer intelligible to posit the view that religion and law are two absolutely opposing antinomies that have no interconnections. Even radical secularists have to admit that religion plays a greater implicit and explicit role in our thinking processes than has hitherto been acknowledged. In the Western tradition two statements were thought to herald the end of religion, Karl Marx's famous and abused characterisation of religion as the 'opium of the masses' and Friedrich Nietzsche's announcement of the 'death of God'. However, by the close of the second millennium 'the classical religions have been neither destroyed nor consigned to folklore,' in the words of Pierre Legendre (Goodrich & Warrington 1990: 3). On the contrary, religion is making an unprecedented reappearance on the world stage.

In some quarters this tendency is viewed with alarm, accompanied by the fear that it may undo the hard-won achievements of post-Enlightenment secularism, especially the achievement of the secular state. On the other hand, for many the emergence of political and social orders in which religion plays a prominent role is viewed as a corrective to the aberrations and havoc that secularism has wrought on society. While the debate on religion and secularism will be briefly dealt with below, I will direct my gaze mainly to law and the effect that religion has had on this pillar of secularism.

Even among the Greeks and the Romans, the progenitors of modern legal systems, law was rooted in the mythic and supernatural world-views of these societies.[1] The fact that law, in its origins, did have religious moorings of some kind is no longer denied. But by the close of the twentieth century, law has 'undisguisedly' become a pragmatic human process and the Siamese twin of the secular order[2] (Berman 1993: 6). The nation-state as a political system has become the symbol of the secular order. Furthermore, secularism and secularisation are no longer exclusively features of Western societies. Colonisation has brought about a semblance of homogenisation of legal and political systems in non-Western cultures in Africa, the Middle East, Asia and Latin America. While each of these contexts is variegated and differentiated, there is in all of them a noticeable tension between what can be characterised as the globalising legal and political order on the one side and the local socio-cultural order on the other. Within non-Western cultures specifically, though not exclusively, this conflict becomes manifest in the debates about democracy which take place when attempts to domesticate imported political systems come into conflict with indigenous values and world-views.

Nowhere else does this encounter of imported legal and political systems with resurgent indigenous socio-legal orders make itself more manifest than in certain Muslim societies, where these debates have assumed fierce proportions. Such debate is also evident, albeit in less spectacular ways, in societies in which African traditional religion, Buddhism or Hinduism are found.[3]

In this essay I will sketch the relationship between religion, state and law in South Africa until the adoption of the 1996 Constitution. Thereafter I will make a close reading of the provisions of 'freedom of religion, belief and opinion' in the overall context of South Africa's new constitutional order. Finally, I will explore some of the implications of this rights discourse for religious communities.

Religion and state in South Africa

South Africa's anti-apartheid struggle received unparalleled support from religious organisations, especially in the last two decades prior to the demise of a political order based on racism. Some of the leading work on liberation theology in Christianity and Islam has emerged from the South African context. One should recall that organised religion has had a long tryst with history in this African sub-region. The European colonial adventures brought with them religion, whether it was the Calvinist brand of Christianity of the Dutch colonists, the Protestantism of the French Huguenots or the Episcopalian variety. Other religions such as Islam, Hinduism and Chinese religious traditions also made their presence felt in this sub-region over a period of roughly three centuries of colonial rule. The indigenous religions of the African peoples were repeatedly denied and demeaned as superstition, syncretism and false religions. Only once European conquest began to succeed in southern Africa around the 1890s did Christian missionaries begin admitting, albeit reluctantly, that indigenous people had a religion (Chidester 1994: 8).

Today, African traditional religion may still be the core religion of the majority of South Africans. However, the mainstream religions, particularly a variety of Christian denominations, prevail over all others in South Africa, both in terms of size and visibility. African traditional religion proper has been eclipsed by the high profile of the African Independent Churches. While the institutional representation of African traditional religion in terms of modern organisation can hardly compete with other religious traditions, it still has a strong following and is showing signs of resurgence. In the past, Christianity defined what was normative with respect to religion, and shaped both colonial policy and that of the apartheid state in this regard. Marginalised religious communities enjoyed no protection from either the state or hegemonic religions. In fact, adherents of Islam and African traditional religion were seen as targets for proselytisation. When the basis of the relationship between the colonial state and its subjects was not one of ethnicity, then it was very often determined by religion.[4] Relationships between religions, if they were not marked by hostility, could be described as competitive. This situation endured for most of South Africa's history until special social circumstances, as well changes within religious traditions in the last two decades of the twentieth century, made inter-religious social action and dialogue possible.

In the 1980s a coalition of Christians, Jews, Muslims, Hindus and Buddhists was formed against apartheid. The representatives of each religious community articulated a social message rooted in their respective religious teachings against the evil of enforced racial separation and tyrannical white rule. It was particularly, though not exclusively, the Christian church that played a leading role in promoting reconciliation.[5] Religion in this sense played a role as both liberator from apartheid ideology and later as facilitator of the transition from apartheid rule to a democratic order by promoting racial reconciliation, most notably between black and white; this has perhaps secured a place for it in the new and emerging post-apartheid political order. Religion has no reason to fear its marginalisation in the new South Africa.

Declaring religious rights and responsibilities: religion anticipates change

Anticipating the emergence of a constitutional state, the religious communities under the auspices of the South African chapter of the inter-religious group called the World Conference on Religion and Peace (WCRP) began to position themselves for the emerging new political order. On 22–24 November 1992 the WCRP held a landmark national inter-faith conference. It was by all accounts the most inclusive religious gathering of its kind ever held in South Africa, and adopted a pre-circulated draft 'Declaration on Religious Rights and Responsibility' that comprised ten principles aimed at regulating the relations among religious communities, as well as relations with the state (WCRP-SA n.d.: 'Affirmation'). A crucial assumption made by the Declaration was that 'these principles will function within the framework of a Bill of Rights' and the conference thus proposed a clause for such a Bill of Rights (BoR). The proposed clause stated:

1. All persons are entitled:
    1.1 to freedom of conscience
    1.2 to profess, practise, and propagate any religion or no religion,
    1.3 to change their religious allegiance.
2. Every religious community and/or member thereof shall enjoy the right:
    2.1 to establish, maintain and manage religious institutions;
    2.2 to have their particular system of family law recognised by the state;
    2.3 to criticise and challenge all social and political structures and policies in terms of the teachings of their religion. (WCRP-SA n.d.: 'Proposed Clause for the Bill of Human Rights')

The Declaration also defined a 'religious community' as 'a group of people who follow a particular system of belief, morality and worship, either in recognition of a divine being, or in pursuit of spiritual development, or in the expression of a sense of belonging through social custom or ritual' (WCRP-SA n.d.: 'We who subscribe to this Declaration', (a)). In the Declaration the signatories acknowledged that religion was 'used to justify injustice, sow conflict and contribute to the oppression, exploitation and suffering of people.' At the same time the signatories recognised that religion also upheld human dignity and justice in the face of oppression. For this reason the representatives of the various religions gathered at Pretoria in 1992, undertook to redress past injustices and committed themselves to the construction of a just society.

A careful observation of the way the religious sector itself defines religion and how that notion became grafted onto the 1996 Constitution will help to illuminate the discussion. 'Religion' in the Declaration is defined as 'belief, morality and worship' in the recognition of a divine being, or in pursuit of spiritual development, or as a sense of expressing one's belonging. In the pursuit of all these rights and responsibilities, the religious communities bound themselves to an 'expression of religion [that] shall not violate the legal rights of others' (WCRP-SA n.d.: Section 1.2). In so doing, religious communities thus affirmed a form of religious freedom that is subject to the surveillance of the law. Religious rights are to be circumscribed by an authority outside of religion. This extra-religious authority or referee is assumed to be the state and its legal apparatus. In the same breath, however, the Declaration asserts that religious communities, singly, jointly or collectively, 'shall have the right to address the state and enter into dialogue on matters important to them'. Any conflict between religion and state is thus to be resolved through 'dialogue'. What the parameters of this dialogue should be, and how it is organised, remain unstated, unless one is to infer a commonsense understanding of the term. The Declaration also states that the religious sector will 'critically evaluate social, economic and political structures and their activities' (WCRP–SA n.d.: Declaration 3.4, 3.5). In a bid to prevent the co-option of religious communities by the state, the Declaration appeals to the religious leadership to 'follow the dictates of their consciences to avoid conspiring or colluding to violate the public good or the legal rights of others' (ibid.).

What becomes evident is that religion, as articulated in the Declaration, sees its future role in the public space as twofold: a passive and private role; and an active and public role. The passive role is to ensure that the rule of law is enforced and that all public activities take place within the framework of legitimacy set by the state. The activist role is limited to the extent that the religious sector will at its discretion invite the state to participate in an undefined mode of dialogue about social and political issues. In terms of this self-understanding of the role of religion in a post-apartheid South Africa, it remains unclear whether civil disobedience on the part of the religious sector, for instance, is an option in the event that dialogue fails. However, the appeal that the Declaration makes to the religious leadership to follow the dictates of conscience in certain instances suggests that protest beyond dialogue may be contemplated. And yet one cannot ignore the fact that, in claiming to be a corrective force and moral conscience of society, the religious sector does envisage a political role for itself. Given the role that religion played in delegitimising power under apartheid, it is understandable that the religious sector should recognise how power is organised as well as identifying its own role in the networks of power in post-apartheid society.

Whatever the religious sector expected on matters of religion in 1992, the new social role and status of religion turned out to be very different in the Bill of Rights (BoR) as contained in the 1996 Constitution. If one reads the Declaration together with the 1996 BoR, the only power that religion can lay claim to is an appeal to the power of morality. It will be remembered that in the Declaration, the religious sector, in some instances, proposed for itself an alternative authority or voice to political authority. There could be several explanations for this gap between expectation and fulfilment. It appears that either the religious sector zealously overestimated its own future role or that the incumbent political powers may not have fulfilled their undisclosed commitments to the religious sector. Less carefully explored is the fact that the religious sector may have overlooked what the possible role of religion would be in a modern state with a liberal, secular and human rights-friendly constitution. In the latter context public expressions of religious beliefs are constitutionally subordinate to the state, and the principles of morality are theorised separately from the domain of politics (see Asad 1993: 206). This raises the question of what conditions and circumstances existed that made it necessary for the Declaration to make such far-reaching claims about the authority of religion in a new democratic order. The reasons why this carefully drafted Declaration did not translate into a suitable legal formulation for consideration by the constitutional writers also need to be explored.

The religious sector was not the only group to have been mobilised by the African National Congress and other pro-democracy forces. Women's groups, trade unions, youth formations, the medical and health-care sector, as well as the education and legal sectors, all produced documents and declarations that would forward their respective visions for a post-apartheid society. From that perspective the religious sector did not have an unusual experience in finding its own vision substantially modified in the BoR. How the vision of these sectional interest groups translated into the norm-setting document of the nation, namely the Constitution, has to be examined elsewhere. Translation is certainly the key metaphor here. How did the vision of the religious sector as set out in the 1992 Declaration translate into the 1996 Constitution? Translation is not a benign act, but a profoundly political one, in so far as it involves a discourse and process of power. In converting the language of religious values, sentiments, visions and dreams into concrete norms, all those involved – from the brokers of religious power to the politicians and constitutional writers – engage in the process of manufacturing the template of power.

The power wielded by the religious community in South Africa is significant. One has to consider the role of the Christian church not only in de-legitimising the apartheid state, but also in baptising the negotiated settlement. The close proximity of crucial members of the religious establishment to the liberation movement prior to the lifting of the ban on the anti-apartheid political parties is an important consideration. With the liberation movement in exile, the religious establishment and the sector of the church and other religions that espoused liberation theology acted as the moral guardians of the anti-apartheid struggle. With the return of the political exiles and the political leadership, the religious establishment in a sense transferred the mantle of moral authority to the politicians. Unfamiliar with the complexity of the vision of the religious establishment for the new society, the politicians only partly incorporated sections of the 1992 Declaration into the final text of the Constitution. Another, less generous explanation could be that the politicians did not share the views of the religious sector and that the Declaration and the process leading up to it were nothing but political posturing, a manifestation of the co-option of the religious sector by the dominant African National Congress alliance. Sceptical as it may sound, this view was not without its supporters. And as the ruling ANC continues to amend its pledges made to the various sectional social charters prior to 1994, this view is increasingly being validated with the benefit of hindsight.

Rethinking religion and the secular in public policy

Before dealing with the specifics of law and religion in the South African context it may be useful to explore briefly the link between religion and public policy. This link is particularly important in the light of the secularisation of the public space in the post-apartheid era. José Casanova has argued that the theory of secularisation should be complex enough to account for the historical contingency that there may be legitimate forms of 'public' religion in the modern world (Casanova 1994: 39). He suggests that the traditional bias against the role of religion in the public domain may be reconsidered in the light of new roles that religion may play. Religion may have a role to play which is not necessarily that of 'positive' societal integration. There are certain expressions of public religion, says Casanova, that do not endanger the modern functional differentiation between the public and the private. In fact the latter may allow for the privatisation of religion on the one hand and the pluralism of subjective religious beliefs on the other.

In order to conceptualise such possibilities, Casanova argues that the secularisation theory will need to reconsider at least three of its historically ethnocentric biases. Firstly, the bias towards subjective Protestant forms and definitions of religion as belonging to the realm of the private. Secondly, the bias towards the liberal conception of politics and what constitutes the public sphere. And, thirdly, the bias towards the sovereign nation-state as the systematic unit of analysis.

By failing to take cognisance of the changing role of religion, and not adequately theorising the notion of the collectivity (of which religion is only one form) we may be denying ourselves a meaningful account of the de-privatisation of religion. The dominant sociology, and the liberal or civic republican models of analysis that make a radical distinction between the public and private, are not very helpful models of analysis. For instance, to say that society is being secularised could imply one or more of several registers of signification. It could mean (a) the differentiation of the secular spheres from religious institutions and norms; (b) the decline of religious beliefs and practices; and (c) the marginalisation of religion by confining it to the private sphere. At the same time, theories of religion or secularisation and modernisation should be open to the idea that there are other kinds of religion that play some role in institutionalising their own patterns of secularisation. Various religious traditions have maintained an uneasy relationship with modernity, partly accommodating and also recognising some of the values of the secular as their own. But these religions refuse to accept the claims of the market as well as those of the state, which suggests that moral norms ought not to interfere in the public space. If carefully considered, the above options as suggested by Casanova could offer a new way of conceptualising religion in public policy in South Africa, different from the conceptualisation discussed in the next section of this essay.

Religion and the 1996 Bill of Rights

The 1996 South African Constitution, more specifically Chapter 2 called the Bill of Rights, does not create a Jeffersonian 'wall of separation between church and state' – the emblematic metaphor for relations between religion and state in modern secular societies. The BoR actually attempts to create what I would call a 'flow' or 'umbilical cord' between state and religion, without establishing a theocracy based on Calvinist principles as the constitution texts of 1961 and 1983 attempted to do (Carpenter 1995: 684). In the preamble to the 1996 Constitution there is a controversial reference to 'God' which some people feel excludes persons who do not adhere to any religion. The controversial part reads, 'May God protect our people. Nkosi Sikelel' iAfrika. ... God bless South Africa.'[6] Persons not affiliated to religion argue that if there is a reference to God, there should also be a reference to some values with which non-religious persons can identify. In this sense the Constitution can be viewed as biased towards theists.

The clause on freedom of religion, belief and opinion in the BoR states:

(1) Everyone has the right to freedom of conscience, religion, thought, belief and opinion.
(2) Religious observances may be conducted at state or state-aided institutions,
provided that
   (a) those observances follow rules made by the appropriate public authorities;
   (b) they are conducted on an equitable basis; and
   (c) attendance at them is free and voluntary.
(3) (a) This section does not prevent legislation recognising
     (i) marriages concluded under any tradition, or a system of religious, personal or family law; or
     (ii) systems of personal and family law under any tradition, or adhered to by persons professing a particular religion.
   (b) Recognition in terms of paragraph (a) must be consistent with this section and the other provisions of the Constitution.

In this section of the BoR standard freedoms are entrenched. However, when it comes to religion, one is only free to hold beliefs, opinions and thoughts. As soon as these freedoms are translated into practice, in the form of religious observances at schools or religion-based family law codes, then such actions are subject to conditions and limitations. It is required that religion in the public domain comply with administrative procedures such as obtaining permission, that it comply with a notion of equitable practice, and be voluntary. All public religious practices must in addition be 'consistent' with the overall thrust of the Constitution and its values. The 1993 Interim Constitution did not explicitly require religious practices to be consistent with the overall constitutional values, but the final text was amended in order to make such a qualification explicit.

A close reading of the BoR discloses a dualistic understanding of religion: religion as belief; and religion as practice. If religion manifests itself as conscience, belief, thought and opinion, in other words as a Cartesian *cogito*, then every citizen has a right to hold such views. In theory, there appears to be absolute freedom in the exercise of religion as an abstract and unarticulated dogma: freedom of religion as the expression of pious intentions. It is, however, debatable whether an abstract freedom can be termed a 'freedom' without its political implications, and also debatable whether anything in the abstract can be termed 'religion'. Can one talk about freedom of religion and thought, if one is not free to speak one's thoughts? Can one talk about religious freedom if one cannot express such belief? (See Mureinik 1994: 34–48, esp. 34.)

On the other hand, the expression of religious practices is subject to the constraints of the 'secular' values of the Constitution. What Section 15 actually achieves is the affirmation of abstract religious freedoms while limiting the freedom to practise religions. Clearly the aim of the limitation is to curb any practice that goes beyond what is 'reasonable and justifiable' (Constitution 1996: Section 36 1) and in so doing undermines the values of 'an open and democratic society based on human dignity, equality and freedom' (ibid.: Section 39 1(a)). There is obviously a huge gulf between the right to believe and the right to manifest such belief. Access to that space is mediated by the constitutional values of dignity, equality and freedom. A more appropriate title for this section of the BoR would have been 'limits to freedom of religion, belief and opinion'.

This dissonance, or rather paradox, between the promise of freedom of religion and the limit on practices occurs because the discourse of freedom of religion has been borrowed from elsewhere and does not reflect the organic texture of the way in which religion is understood and practised in South Africa. The rhetorical pedigree of the 1996 BoR is transparent. Its genealogical affiliation is to post-Enlightenment European thought, not post-colonial Africa. The fundamental freedoms of religion in the European context arise out of a quest for freedom from a particular kind of religious oppression and denial, which also entailed a move towards the plurality of religious belief. The same can also be said about the United States of America (USA). In fact, the disestablishment of religion in the USA was meant to protect religion from state interference and not to create hostility between religion and state (see Carter 1993).

It is not very difficult to grasp the presumptions and assumptions that the authors of the Constitution make about religion. The working assumption is very much a post-Reformation one, which distinguishes between the public and the private, the secular and the profane (see Sullivan 1994: 37). In this discourse, religion is primarily a private concern. So what may appear to be the privileging of religion, in the rhetorical phrase 'freedom of religion', actually only means the freedom to practise religion in the realm of the private, not the public. Stated differently, one can say that freedom of religion means the restriction and limitation to have jurisdiction in only a narrow set of activities.

What this means is that when religious practices are offensive to the secular constitutional values, but not necessarily devoid of moral insight, the abstract notion of freedom is erased, and a form of civic republicanism would deem these religious acts to be illegal. For liberals, religious belief worthy of respect depends on its mode of acquisition. From a political point of view, if religious belief and practice have the tendency to promote the habits and dispositions that make good citizens or promote the good life but conflict with some of the other constitutional values, such religion would be deemed offensive in South Africa. Polygyny is a good example of this. If this practice, which is sanctioned by religion, does not inhibit the making of good citizens, but may conflict with an interpretation of gender equality, would polygyny then be deemed offensive on these grounds? Most probably yes, in terms of the liberal doctrine of constitutionalism. The problem raised here is not so much whether society should or should not be protected from offensive and degrading behaviour from whatever quarter, including religion. The issue is a more fundamental one: the misrepresentation of religious rights in South African constitutional discourse, which gestures towards an absolute freedom by the invocation of the phrase 'freedom of religion' but does not necessarily fulfil that pledge. At the same time, the legal regulation of religion does not necessarily reflect the social practices and expectations of a very diverse religious community.

Another feature of the 1996 constitutional text is the complete omission of any reference to *ubuntu*, the value of African humanism which constituted one of the philosophical strands that informed the 1993 Interim Constitution. In fact, the reference to *ubuntu* was a positive feature since it at least acknowledged that African tradition and values would inform the interpretation of an otherwise extremely Eurocentric legal system. The postamble to the 1993 Constitution stated that 'there is a need for understanding but not for vengeance, a need for reparation but not for retaliation, a need for *ubuntu* but not for victimisation'. In a major ruling abolishing the death penalty, the Constitutional Court in *S v. Makwanyane* made reference to *ubuntu* as one of the values that informed the BoR. A great deal was made of the positive contribution of indigenous and organic values to the overall legal system. The omission of *ubuntu* must therefore mean that the Constitution was de-Africanised in the re-drafting process. With that the religio-cultural values of African people are also devalued. Thus the desire to formulate a core legal system which encapsulates the multiple value systems in South Africa was not necessarily accomplished in the final Constitution.

Metaphysics of law and rights

Juridical categories, Legendre tells us, do not conceal within themselves their own justification.

> They are juridical categories only because they are founded in, that is to say they refer to, the principle of division from which they spring. The Tiers of juridical categories ... the founding Reference ... are dealing with the theatrical character of institutions. In every society the basic founding discourse is a celebration, a ritualisation, because it is a matter of bringing alive, on a social scale, the representation of the foundations, the representation of that which renders the function of the categories conceivable. (Goodrich & Warrington 1990: 7–8)

It appears that society organises itself on the basis of representation. This representation takes place through theatre, as Legendre points out, of which political dramatisation, music, song or rituals are the media for the enactment of totemic truth. Whether we call it metaphysics, myth or cosmology, even legal systems and legal institutions contain elements of these hidden components from which they derive their justification. This is what is meant by the French term 'tiers', which refers to an external third element that is outside juridical categories.

Not only religion is an enactment of totemic truth; so is the Constitution. The combination of or the tension between religion and political–legal categories enhances the complexity of these truths. While the Constitution is mainly a guide for political conduct and reflects on the authority of legal language, it does introduce religious themes at crucial points, such as the reference to a theism in the words 'May God protect our people' and 'God bless South Africa'. The ecumenical thrust of the Constitution, for want of a better term, appears to espouse inclusivity, healing, reconciliation, human dignity, equality, freedom and the redress of past injustices. In other words, it speaks in a sense the language of justice and the theology of reconciliation under the watchful guise of a nondescript theism. But these same terms also have another register of meaning. The terms freedom, equality and openness employed in the Constitution are framed in the language of rights – the language of modern political theory and law. These contending 'meanings' – ethical, religious, legal, political or even eudaemonic – are thematic categories that are torn apart by the perplexing difficulty (*aporia*) that constitutes each.

Paul de Man (following his close reading of Rousseau's *Social Contract*) believes that a constitutional document describes two things: firstly, the ideal state, which is its constative aspect; and, secondly, the legal acts of the state, which are its performative aspect. The system of relationships that generates the text, not its referential meaning, is what De Man calls the grammar or logical code of the constitutional text (De Man 1979: 268). The grammar or logical code of such a text is only conceivable by suspending its referential meaning. By this he means the immediacy which the code has to a very specific instance and consequence. This is different from Legendre's term 'tiers', which defines 'reference' as a mythical referential point. For this reason, to return to De Man, a law must be written by suspending its applicability to a particular entity, in the same way that the grammatical logic of the constitution can only function if its referential consequences are disregarded. Paradoxically, we also know that law ceases to be if it is not applicable to particular individuals. It is only when law refers to a particular praxis that the justice of the law can be tested. Justice is always realised in a very particular instance. An individual citizen always desires the well-being of each and everyone, while secretly appropriating the word *each* for himself or herself.

> There can be no text without grammar: the logic of grammar generates texts only in the absence of referential meaning, but every text generates a referent that subverts the grammatical principle to which it owed its constitution. What remains hidden in the everyday use of language, the fundamental incompatibility between grammar and meaning, becomes explicit when the linguistic structures are stated, as is the case here, in political terms. ... The incompatibility between the elaboration of the law and its application (or justice) can only be bridged by an act of deceit. (De Man 1979: 269)

The constative and performative aspects of the Constitution are in permanent tension. In the gap between the grammar of the Constitution and its applications, legal history evolves. New and varied legal acts and interpretations are attributed to the original text by means of the rhetorical figure of metalepsis, the trope that reverses cause and effect through the shuttling of priorities. By means of the rhetoric of metalepsis, current decisions are legitimised as the choices of the legal tradition or as the necessary or correct interpretation of the legal texts. Any legislative text that attempts to reconcile the conflicting requirements of a discourse of politics, justice and truth is prone to such metalepsis.

Implicit in the framing of religious rights is a binarism which contrasts religion with non-religion, the private with the public and the secular with the profane. In so far as the practices of religion or religious persons conform to the overall values of the Constitution, there is a symmetry in the reason of the individual (*logos*) and the reason of the state (*nomos*). The constitutional text makes the assumption that the individual and the state are reconciled in their values and in the reason of the law. It may be too early to predict, but there are very few indications that the new South African Constitution has incorporated the consensus values of the majority community. In making the (false) assumption of the reconciliation of the individual or community with the reason of the law, the Constitution arrives at the metaphor of Western metaphysics, *logos* reconciled with *nomos*. 'A perfect harmony is thus attained in the realisation that we are puppets of a good puppeteer in whose game we participate (life is a patterned nomological play)' (Douzinas et al. 1991: 91). In the metaphor of logonomocentrism, 'the claim of the unity of self and others in absolute reason of the law' is made. Logonomocentrism promises the truth of reason and the reason of law, which are both games of figurality and rhetoricity. If, however, there is asymmetry between the practices of religious persons and the reason of the state (*nomos*), then the only way logonomocentrism deals with these relations is to 'other' and delegitimise these practices as aberrant and illegal.

What the Constitution does is to retain the fiction of the sovereignty of religion, whereas the logic of modernity, and liberalism in particular, has long since eroded this in practice. It retains the pretence of this sovereignty by the invocation of the rhetoric of freedom of religion. But in reality it is a freedom which finds its limits in the logic of the state.

The problematic part of this kind of constitutional formulation is that it creates the expectation of religious freedom, but in effect allows the state to interfere with religion. There is only one sovereign, which is the state, although lawyers would argue that in South Africa the Constitution is sovereign. However, one has to acknowledge that constitutional sovereignty is largely in the service of the state. If one takes the example of religion, then constitutional guarantees for freedom of religion are reduced to expressions of the will of the state. Religion in South Africa is without a doubt more vulnerable to legislative and judicial interference than religion in the United States, where the proverbial wall of separation exists between religion and the state. The partnership between religion and state in South Africa, as some would describe it, reduces religion to the status of 'junior partner'. There are no clauses which protect religion from the caprice of the state. The possibility of religion being co-opted by the state is infinitely greater, despite the wishes of the authors of the Declaration to the contrary. At least within the constitutional system of the USA, the state is prohibited from establishing any religion or legally interfering with religion. In South Africa the state can establish any religion, provided it can justify such procedures as fulfilling the requirements of administrative propriety and equality. This opens the way for the co-option of religion and diminishes the possibility for the prophetic voice of religion to be heard in a critique of the state. While it is possible to co-opt religion in the USA, this cannot be done in a legal manner without skilful subterfuge. In South Africa, such co-option can be achieved with constitutional sanction. In the USA religion would have to translate itself into a secular and pragmatic system of values and cease to be religion, before it could legally play a role in legislation and the affairs of state. In South Africa values can theoretically be incorporated with their religious peculiarities intact, provided that the state approves of them.

Conclusion

South Africa has adopted a liberal constitution in which religion is subordinate to state authority. The paradox in the South African context lies in the dissonance between the aspirations of the religious communities and the lack of any legal and political means to realise these aspirations. At least constitutionally, religion is coerced to operate within the language of rights and will, willingly or unwillingly, shape a rights-bearing citizen. But religion also sees itself as a normative discourse whose purpose includes the making of a virtuous citizen. The question of duty is an important requirement in a nascent democracy like South Africa, with its myriad social and economic challenges. The debate between rights and duty in political culture is far from resolved, and remains a contentious area of concern.

The post-apartheid South African state is moving towards a monolithic culture of secular legal morality, if the excision of non-secular values and references in the new Constitution is anything to go by. Inclusivity, transparency and openness do not necessarily mean the possibility of multiple moral references. The Constitution may be tolerant of multiple moral centres, as long as these do not threaten the emerging rights-centred juro-moral authority. In the final analysis, the state will dictate its own secular moral register.

The BoR, as part of the Constitution, could have been lifted out of any European setting, even though there is great excitement about its being one of the most advanced and liberal documents of its kind. As previously indicated, this normative document lacks an indigenous moral foundation and a rootedness in local culture. It is difficult to see how and where the values and culture of the African majority resonate in this text, except through rapid acculturation and subordination to a Eurocentric juristic culture. The BoR has its moral foundations in the universal reason of a rights culture, and the extent of its compatibility with a culture that furthers the cause of a disciplined and virtuous citizen is unknown.

The advent of constitutional governance in South Africa is bound to impact on the transformation of religion. It is also heralds the success of the modern state in the grand narrative of cultural transformation accompanied by the rise of modern industrial societies and globalisation. Cultural transformation means the decline of religion in industrialised societies and the progressive secularisation of beliefs and practices as well as the rationalisation of social life. So, while premodern forms of religion and magic lose their hold over societies, we witness the proliferation of newer forms of religion and religious institutions through mass communications and networks of transmission by means of which commodified symbolic forms, religion included, are made available to larger and greater audiences.

What happens in South Africa, as elsewhere, is that religion is mediated through a range of symbolic forms, in law, politics, economics and culture. Religion as a symbolic form is embedded in structured social contexts involving relations of power, forms of conflict and inequalities. Despite its symbolic manifestation, we know that within social contexts religion becomes the object of complex processes of valuation, evaluation and conflict – what J. B. Thompson calls the process of valorisation as ideology. (Thompson 1990: 12).

Chapter Seven

The African customary law of marriage and the rights conundrum

Thandabantu Nhlapo

South African society is undergoing very rapid transformation on many fronts. Indeed, for many people the function of the government is defined in terms of change; of overturning the old order and establishing the structures and institutions that will underpin a new one. The formal authority for all this activity is of course the Constitution. Away from the official arena that same document has concentrated the minds of many ordinary South Africans on what transformation means for them in their daily lives. Employers and employees, educators and students, leaders and followers, service providers and clients, players and spectators, are all still groping for a working relationship that takes into account the plain fact that in the new South Africa it cannot be 'business as usual'.

In all this jockeying for position (because that is what it is), it is sometimes forgotten that some of the most important relationships to be negotiated are, unfortunately, also the relationships over which the past casts the longest shadows. I would classify in this category all those relationships which have ethnicity or culture at their centre. With the best will in the world, it still appears to be uncommonly difficult in South Africa today to discuss any matter which involves the interests represented by the indigenous world-view (if such a thing exists) and the 'received' value system (if such a thing exists) with any degree of objectivity and impartiality. The arena of justice and rights is as good an example of this difficulty as any.

Justice and rights and the problem with 'rights talk'

Ordinarily the notion of human rights should be seen as playing an important supportive role in efforts aimed at the achievement of social justice. Another way of putting this would be to say that the acknowledgement that the citizens of a country are holders of rights which are opposable against other citizens and against the state should be an important component in the promotion of a just society. And at this stage one does not necessarily require a highly theoretical definition of 'just' or 'justice'. The ordinary South African does have a working definition of these concepts, namely anything that is an improvement on the apartheid past, which was universally acknowledged to be 'unjust'.

The notion of 'rights', on the other hand, presents a problem in a number of ways:

(i) There is a problem with ordinary perceptions of what is meant by a right, and confusion as to who is entitled to what. At this level people routinely take more than their share, believing 'right' to mean 'what I want to do'.

(ii) A different problem of public perception is sometimes inadvertently promoted by officialdom itself, when rights are offered or granted (or advertised) without due emphasis on correlative obligations – thus encouraging a culture of entitlement – as if there could ever be entitlement in a vacuum.

(iii) Then there is of course the classical problem of a legitimate clash between two or more rights – that is, even where there exists no misconception about the meaning of 'right'. In these cases emphasis on one right necessarily harms the other, and a balancing act is required to make sense of the co-existence of both.

(iv) The really significant difficulty, though, with 'rights talk' is the perception that its particular history and origins place it squarely in the Western value system – that is, the human rights discourse when it is wearing its international United Nations cap.[1] It is often not sufficiently realised that this is a huge problem, if the intention is to make human rights 'stick in societies newly arrived in the self-government game. These are societies over which the hand of authority was so heavy in the past that the habit of acting independently as moral agents (in the legal arena, at least) has not developed fully amongst the majority of the population. If a 'culture of rights' (currently a popular phrase in South Africa) is to take root in such a society – and in a sustainable fashion – the association of human rights with Western thought and a Western world-view in the minds of the general populace does not help. It simply clutters up an already acrimonious debate when disapproval of selected aspects of 'Western' culture seeps into the area of human rights as well.

One may expand on this last point by noting several factors which contribute to the difficulty. The first must surely be the prestige or 'clout' that is carried by the movement sometimes characterised in university curricula as International Protection of Human Rights. There is no doubt that from the Universal Declaration onwards it has been impossible to ignore the immense moral weight of the United Nations-driven international human rights system.

Widely ratified instruments such as the Convention on the Elimination of All Forms of Discrimination Against Women and the Convention on the Rights of the Child simply underline the nature of that system as embodying an international moral consensus on issues of minimum standards of treatment for human beings.

How can such a positive state of affairs be a problem? It can be a problem when the movement is made to perform like a juggernaut, sweeping all in its path and brooking no opposition. 'Opposition' is itself a problematic word to use. Subjectively, one who questions any aspect of the international human rights movement may not be intending to 'oppose' at all, merely to understand or fine-tune, or explore the possibilities of accommodation between competing interests. In a national debate, one might for example question whether the ratifying of a particular convention would not amount to the importation of expectations that in practice would be difficult or impossible to fulfil in any number of contexts: Third World, poor, rural, non-Christian, drought-stricken, war-torn or other specific situations. Zealous defenders of human rights have been known to be scathing about such mere questioning, quick to characterise the questioner as 'uncivilised' or 'reactionary'.[2]

Closely allied to the problem discussed above is the fear of human rights activists that if one tampers with even the smallest part of the structure, the whole house of cards will come tumbling down. This is the 'slippery slope' argument: if you allow a deviation from a well-known and well-loved right such as that of non-discrimination, how soon will you find yourself back in the bad old days of slavery, racism, sexism and so on?

A third defect inherent in the strength and popularity of the human rights movement is the failure of some of its proponents to distinguish between ends and means. Human rights are then accorded some superior, almost mystical status, and their original role as a means to the laudable end of justice for all is forgotten. At this point the movement ceases to interrogate itself as to what makes for a *better* world: the assumption is simply made that the accumulated wisdom of 'civilised nations' has finally got it right – we *know* what a better world is; it is one that has attributes (a), (b) and (c), which are themselves uncontested. In multicultural contexts this 'cocksureness' is as much a threat to justice as is the rhetoric of despots who are genuine enemies of human rights.

Multiculturalism

Ordinarily, multiculturalism ought to refer to the right of a people to retain their cultural identity (linguistic, religious, social and so on) even in a political state concerned with the creation and promotion of an overarching national identity.

That it is a right may possibly be debatable in abstract terms: in the concrete terms of South Africa's positive law it is not. Sections 30, 31 and 15 of the Constitution grant these rights expressly.

Section 30 provides that everyone has the right to use the language and to participate in the cultural life of their choice. Section 31(1) says:

> Persons belonging to a cultural, religious or linguistic community may not be denied the right, with other members of their community, to
> (a) enjoy their culture, practise their religion and use their language; and
> (b) form, join and maintain cultural, religious and linguistic association and other organs of civil society.

After granting 'everyone' the right to freedom of conscience, religion, thought, belief and opinion in Section 15(1), the Constitution makes a significant concession to family law in Section 15(3):

> This section does not prevent legislation recognising
> (i) marriage concluded under any tradition or a system of religious, personal or family law; or
> (ii) systems of personal and family law under any tradition or adhered to by persons professing a particular religion.

The Bill of Rights thus complies with the injunction found in Principle XI of the Interim Constitution, which required the framers of the new Constitution to protect and promote linguistic and cultural diversity.

A word about culture

The meaning which I attribute to the term 'culture' in this discussion is influenced by the views of those scholars who find it more useful to talk about what culture *does* than to struggle to define what it is.[3] Thus when R. M. Keesing (1976: 137) refers to culture as a system of shared ideas and meanings 'that underlie the ways in which people live' he underscores an important use of culture – that is, as a device which enables us to give meaning to the world, to make statements to one another about ourselves and about the universe.[4]

In South African discourse there is a noticeable intellectual reluctance to acknowledge the existence of different cultures, even in the broad sense. This appears to stem partly from an appreciation that what we term 'culture' has a history and that in this country that history has involved a political agenda which led directly to apartheid. There is also unease about the idea that culture is uniquely associated with a single society or nation (Thornton 1988: 20–3). 'Culture' is thus viewed with suspicion as being either too vague in content to be useful as a scientific category or simply undesirable in a society still displaying the scars of enforced differentiation.

Given the evil legacy that orthodox views of culture bequeathed to South Africa, such reluctance is understandable. However, in the urge to refute the thinking which fed the foundations of segregation, modern scholarship seems to be having at least one confusing side effect. It resonates with images of a kind of cultural facelessness which, to many African people in particular, presages an unwelcome vacuum in the area of social identity. This intellectual tradition appears to be uncomfortable with the use of 'culture' in broad distinctions such as 'African' and 'Western' culture, which is viewed as being somewhat racist. To my mind, this is overly cautious. As long as we are careful to specify what we mean there appears to be no harm in using 'African' and 'Western' as convenient categories in advancing a particular argument.

To assert the existence of an African culture is not to promote claims of its superiority over other cultures, nor is it to suggest that only Africans can participate in it or that none of its items overlap with, or are replicated in, the cultural packages of others. Similarly, the label 'Western culture' need not imply a judgement of value or acknowledge the sanctity of the boundaries of such culture. The fact that we are all able to participate, across boundaries, in one another's cultural repertoire does not to my mind compel conclusion that the labels themselves are meaningless (Nhlapo 1992: 5–14).

It is possible to detect a subjective element in the process of constructing a sense of belonging. One invariably has the opportunity of emphasising or de-emphasising one's membership in the many identities which may have a claim on one's allegiance. Thus, if I raise my children in a particular way, which is different from my neighbour's, I may believe that it is because I am African (or Christian or Zulu) or because I have had a formal education (or a history of deprivation, or a rural upbringing) and so on. What I choose to believe or reject from among these options will surely be influenced by what else I believe about myself and about life. This element of 'volition' seems to be at the heart of belonging. People must believe that it is important for them to be one thing and not another.[5]

The foregoing discussion already hints at the difficulties inherent in any attempt to transform social attitudes and behaviours. Surely the precise problem with the use of the term 'culture', as Ngubane (1991) notes, is that no distinction is made between its various components:

(i) preferred forms of greeting, modes of dress, aesthetic activities and leanings, yearning for familiar ways, and so on;

(ii) basic values and interpretations of nature and society;

(iii) the organising principles of society.

There are many others: the important point about them is that some may change or may be given up quite easily. You begin to know a people when you start to understand how readily they will change, or how firmly they will resist an attempt to make them depart from any part of what they perceive as their culture. This is an important distinction: between the more superficial and the deeper levels of culture; the readily changeable parts and the durable ones, or what Professor Ngubane calls the hardware and the software. It may be difficult to define but a few illustrations do come to mind.

It may be easy to give up modes of dress and greeting; it may not be so easy to adopt a whole new view of what it means to be a person (personhood). Similarly, aesthetic values and musical or artistic practices may change over time; not so methods of dealing with life's crises, such as birth or death. Such a distinction explains the tenacity of certain practices in the face of changing social contexts.

African family law as a cultural right

When the provisions found in Sections 15, 30 and 31 are read together, a strong argument can be made that the African customary law of the family is specifically recognised in the South African Constitution, together with systems of personal law based on any religion. It is true that any law recognising these regimes must ensure that such recognition is consistent with the Constitution. African family law acquires its clear constitutional position not only from Section 15 but also from Section 211(3) which reads: 'The courts must apply customary law when that law is applicable, subject to the Constitution and any legislation that specifically deals with customary law.'

A question that arises is whether customary law in general and customary family law in particular can be made to ride on the coat-tails, as it were, of Sections 30 and 31, which recognise a person's right to 'participate in' or 'enjoy' his or her culture. In terms of the definition of culture discussed earlier, there is no doubt that a people's laws and legal system qualify as an important part of that people's cultural package (see also Bennett 1995: 23–4). This is probably even more true of indigenous systems of law, which are sometimes so intertwined with other cultural and social institutions as to be indistinguishable as separate entities. If this is true, then the right of various communities across the country to be governed by their own systems of personal law – namely, the customary law of the family – finds recognition in the Constitution not only in those provisions recognising customary law but in those recognising culture as well.

The difficulties inherent in this kind of constitutional recognition of culture are well known: the potential for conflict between some cultural institutions and practices, on the one hand, and the Bill of Rights, on the other, are well documented (see, for example, Bennett 1993: 269; 1995: 80; and Kaganas and Murray 1994: 409).

Those conflicts specifically involving African customary law have also received a lot of attention. For the purposes of this discussion, it will suffice to sketch in brief the nature of customary family law, and point out those areas where the application of a human rights yardstick might produce some tension.

The African customary law of the family is the outward and visible sign of a very deep and all-pervasive conception of the world and the meaning of life. It is a view of the world as a place where life's imperatives are survival and security, values which have spawned a maze of elaborate mechanisms for their achievement. By far the most central and durable of these is kinship and the institution of the family. It is impossible to exaggerate the importance of kinship in the African psyche – education and modernisation notwithstanding.[6] The configurations, ceremonies and rituals found in the elaborate process of marriage are testimony to the importance that Africans attach to the formation of families. These practices have over time acquired pride of place amongst many groups as the single most important feature of their identity. Suppression by both the colonial and the apartheid state has merely served to kindle a passionate allegiance to these 'badges of difference' by the people who participate in them.

The configurations within African family law include polygyny,[7] a classificatory form of kinship,[8] and various kinds of social parenthood.[9] Most rituals and ceremonies revolve around the negotiation and transfer of lobolo[10] between the two kinship groups and involve slaughtering, feasting and play-acting. Anybody with the time to spare can find in this complex cultural package countless examples of sex-based divisions: 'boys only' and 'girls only' activities, 'women only' and 'men only' ceremonies. The scrutineer will also find plenty of inequality: indeed, fundamentally the whole relationship is predicated on the pre-eminent position of the bride's family as the holders of the 'prize' and the 'cap in hand' situation of the groom's family as the seekers of that prize. It does not take much imagination to realise that this centrepiece of African culture – namely, family law – which will no doubt be defended fiercely in case of attack, is also the one most vulnerable to challenges from a human rights standpoint. In a sense this essay is about whether those challenges are always justified and well directed.

Unequal cultures and the language of rights

History abounds with examples of misunderstanding arising from the juxtaposition of peoples with not merely different, but divergent, cultures. In Africa the problem has tended to be that from the earliest contact with Europeans the two cultural blocs involved in the contact have never enjoyed a position of equality. The Europeans, believing in the unquestioned superiority of their own moral, religious, political and legal institutions, lost no time in suppressing various aspects of African culture by law and by force. This was to set in motion a process of 'othering'[11] of African institutions that remains relatively intact to the present.

Current debate in South Africa has so far failed to narrow the gap: condemnation of African practices may be less strident but still appears to emanate from the same launching pad, namely an instinctive preference for that which bears some resemblance to familiar Western forms. With the possible exception of a few scholars to whom a deep understanding of the African value system seems important, much of the condemnation appears to come from people with little real understanding of African culture and, sadly, with no intention of attaining such understanding.[12] This is doubly discouraging because it shows no movement from the situation which obtained in the early days of the 'new dispensation'. In 1991, concerned about a general lack of interest among some South Africans in African culture except to criticise it, I wrote urging us all as South Africans not only to learn about 'the others' and what is important to them, but also to be prepared to question our own orthodoxies. I posed the question: 'One may well ask: what does this do for us? What purpose is served by dancing around the issues, pretending understanding for practices that strike us instinctively as abhorrent? Indeed, is that not patronising?' And I answered it thus: 'Making an effort to understand the deep culture of others enhances our credibility. It pulls the carpet from under the feet of anyone who seeks to argue that our secret agenda is to impose our own standards on others without being ourselves willing to adopt new modes of thinking. It "disinfects" the platform from which we wish to launch social criticisms' (see Nhlapo 1991).

That was in 1991. The words appear to have even more relevance today when the debate has been made more concrete by the inclusion in the Constitution of protection both for human rights and for culture.

Western culture is powerful, transportable and all-pervasive. It would be a miracle if this strength did not seep into all manner of discourse in national life – social, economic and political. When this culture claims a family tie with the international human rights movement (a plausible and legitimate claim, sometimes), the danger increases that a non-Western culture will be marginalised by arguments which, among others, now include the rights dimension. It makes possible a three-step shift which goes something like: (i) we do not understand your kinship system; (ii) your kinship system is so different from ours that it is a cause for concern; (iii) your kinship system violates human rights. It then becomes crucially important, when assessing the criticism, to discover if the final conclusion has anything to do with the earlier steps, or can objectively stand alone.

This leads to an important insight into the problems inherent in the language of rights. It is language capable of being deployed in defence of privilege, rightly enough, but not necessarily in the way we might think. Debates about culture tend to start off from the premise that culture is to be viewed with suspicion because it often masks inequality. Claims to a *right* to culture are scrutinised and analysed to show that they are invariably made by the privileged in society (ruling elites or beneficiaries of the patriarchal order, for instance) to the detriment of the *individual* rights of others, for example workers or women. While this is undoubtedly true in many cases, it is often overlooked that there is another level at which human rights talk may be deployed: that is, by the privileged in a wider national sense. One has, in effect, concentric circles of privilege where one's pre-eminent position in one's own sphere is overshadowed by the pre-eminence of someone else operating in their sphere, which happens to be wider.

I am certainly more privileged than the people whose lives under customary law I write about, in the sense that I can, for example, widen the reach of my views by having them published in English nationally and abroad. When we organise officially into political parties and lobby groups we are even more powerful and privileged, having the ear of national newspaper chains and television talk shows.

Keeping in mind what was said earlier, it is clear that the language of rights can be used in these conditions to defend a different kind of privilege. Specifically, it can be used to legitimise pressures on indigenous communities to adopt ways more consonant with the sensibilities of elites, pressures which would have been dismissed as ethnocentric only a few decades ago. Thus, for instance, while conceding that the missionaries got it wrong and *lobolo* is not wife purchase, a person for whom the practice has always rankled now has a second bite at the cherry: that is, to attack the practice on the basis of one or other of the provisions of the Bill of Rights.

This is not necessarily illegitimate: all practices must now be tested against the Constitution. It is the purpose of the test that is important. One can see either a genuine attempt to make multiculturalism work (a process requiring genuine tolerance of difference), or an implacable resistance to living with any cultural variation that is unfamiliar to the received value system. If the human rights argument is enlisted with regard to the latter project, I would submit that this would be in defence of privilege – the privilege of elites who, having internalised the values of modernisation and Westernisation, are unwilling to share moral space with alternative models of living.

Sometimes I believe that we as scholars are occasionally guilty of sleight-of-hand here. We applaud the attribute of culture that we call 'dynamic, not static', but we seem to have our eye fixed firmly on a particular result of such dynamism. That is to say, we expect the end product to be 'progressive'; to conform to some ideal that we have in mind. For instance, we may be happy to leave indigenous cultures alone, secure in the knowledge that slowly they will become more like us – literate, ambitious, mortgaged to the hilt and, above all, fully clothed. We may not say it, but we have a firm idea of the kind of butterfly we would like to see bursting out of the cocoon. One wonders how benignly we would continue to look at a culture's ability to find its own level if there were no guarantees that the end product would meet with our approval. If this even vaguely touches upon the truth, are we not then in danger of recognising (albeit unconsciously) as rights only the interests of those with whom we agree, or of supporting and promoting only those processes where the outcome meets with our approval?

Resolving the conflicts: a job for the courts

The recognition of a right to culture in the Constitution is, unfortunately, only the beginning of the debate, not the end. Rights to culture have to be given life in the context of the day-to-day realities of contemporary South Africa. In the first place, the grant of rights is itself hedged in with the requirement that these rights are to be enjoyed only when they are not in conflict with either the Constitution generally or the Bill of Rights in particular. Thus, the right to language and culture in Section 30 may not be exercised 'in a manner inconsistent with any provision of the Bill of Rights'. The same formula qualifies the rights in Section 31 in relation to cultural, linguistic and religious communities (Section 31 (2)). The recognition of religious, personal and family laws is restricted by the requirement that such recognition must be 'consistent with other provisions in the Constitution' (Section 15 (3)(b)).

Anyone claiming a right to some cultural observance or practice must therefore be satisfied that such observance or practice is constitutionally 'clean'. The issue of onus is not clear here. The only guideline that exists is found in Section 9(5) and relates to the right to non-discrimination: 'discrimination is unfair unless it is established to be fair'. Clearly, if a cultural or religious practice is invoked as a right, the one who asserts it must prove that where it discriminates between people it does not do so unfairly. It is not clear that the same onus would rest on anyone asserting a practice which was challenged on grounds other than discrimination (for instance, that it restricts freedom of movement). But even the test in relation to discrimination is difficult to apply. It throws everything back onto the word 'fair', which means 'just'. The right not to be discriminated against thus aims at achieving justice – which may yet imply recourse to culturally determined notions of what is just.

One may of course also create some space for the operation of a particular cultural practice by invoking Section 36, the limitation clause. Any limitation of a right guaranteed in the Bill of Rights can be pursued by law only if the limitation 'is reasonable and justifiable in an open and democratic society based on human dignity, equality and freedom'. A court assessing whether a limitation is reasonable and justifiable will have to consider, among other factors:

    (a) the nature of the right;

    (b) the importance of the purpose of the limitation;

    (c) the nature and extent of the limitation;

    (d) the relation between the limitation and its purpose; and

    (e) less restrictive means to achieve the purpose.

The third, and potentially most productive approach, is to enlist the aid of the human dignity argument. There is no need to reopen the debates generated by Rhoda Howard and Jack Donnelly on cultural relativism (see for example Donnelly 1982: 76; Donnelly & Howard 1986: 801–17). One can simply make straight for an argument which suggests that the demands of human dignity might themselves provide a reason for enforcing rights to a particular identity opposable to the claims of some wider national identity.[13] And therein lies the conundrum. If it is an important component of human dignity to hold religious beliefs, to worship and to be devout, how is a constitution based on the three pillars of human dignity, equality and freedom to deal with a religion according to the tenets of which women, say, cannot conduct ceremonies that male church leaders conduct?

If certain configurations and rituals are central to a particular people's kinship system, without which they feel a low sense of self-worth (and therefore a low sense of dignity), how is the same constitution to protect their dignity in the face of condemnation by non-members citing human rights arguments? These are not easy questions, but perhaps a closer examination of the argument based on human dignity may yield a solution.

One of the advantages of adopting the standard of human dignity as the bridge between contemporary notions of rights and African traditional culture lies in the fact that the Interim Constitution itself acknowledges dignity as a right to be protected. In Article 10 the Constitution provides: 'Every one has inherent dignity and the right to have their dignity respected and protected.' This opens the way for the courts to incorporate this standard in practical ways when faced with competing systems of values.

This is not to suggest that the standard will be easy to apply. The difficulties become apparent when one considers the controversies surrounding activities such as the sport of midget-tossing. Concerned citizens may want the sport outlawed because it offends their sense of propriety to see an adult man used as a missile to determine which player can toss him the furthest. They would argue that this is undignified. The midgets involved may turn around and defend the sport as their means of livelihood, arguing essentially: 'If we do not mind, why should you?' It does not take a great leap of the imagination to conceive of similar considerations arising when the issue of the constitutionality of *lobolo*, for instance, or polygyny comes before the Constitutional Court. In matters involving dignity is it ever possible to go beyond the subjective views of the person concerned?

I submit that the devices available to the court will involve two kinds of considerations. Firstly the court can, in a technical sense, insert the concept of dignity into constitutional interpretation at various points. Thus, in interpreting Article 9(3) it may find that the different treatment of people on the basis of sex does not constitute *unfair* discrimination so long as it is not a breach of human dignity. The scope of the rights guaranteed in that article would thus depend crucially on the court's understanding of dignity. In the same way the human dignity implications may be used as a yardstick to determine whether a measure which purports to limit a fundamental right is 'reasonable and justifiable' within the meaning of Article 36(1).

The second kind of consideration is more abstract. Here the court would have to apply its mind to balancing the explicit protection of culture in Articles 15, 30 and 31 with the demands of the equality provision. It would have to confront head-on questions such as whether the equality principle requires the introduction of an artificial even-handedness in every transaction, so that criticisms of polygyny would be addressed, for example, by allowing a woman to have more than one husband.

Here the best way of deploying the human dignity test would be to realise that there may be conceptions of human dignity that are distinctly African; that where a woman tells us that she feels 'valued' by having her husband's family negotiate *lobolo* with her father, we should be reluctant to substitute our own beliefs about her situation, dismissing hers.

At the end of the day this will involve an acknowledgement that the Bill of Rights should be the locus for a newly negotiated value system for our country: in such an exercise it is only fair that the competing world-views and cultural packages start out as at least notionally equal. Where it cannot be conclusively shown that a particular cultural practice is worse than a competing one, the decision to prefer the one over the other should not depend on an assertion of the general moral superiority of the value system of a particular group in society.

Conclusion

This discussion has attempted to raise awareness of one aspect of the human rights discourse which receives little attention in debate. This is when the United Nations-based international human rights movement is harnessed to the value system that may loosely be termed 'Western' and, in that role, is used to attack certain non-Western behaviours and practices, thus blurring the real motive for the criticism. It is not being suggested that 'international' criticism of local practices is always illegitimate: no strong cultural relativism is being asserted here.[14] Rather, the argument is advanced that, where the contending cultures do not enjoy equality of status, the danger increases that in its criticism of local circumstances the dominant culture will be tempted to enlist the prestige of the international human rights movements to mask a basic intolerance of competing world-views.

The discussion suggests that the area of African family law is especially vulnerable because its institutions and practices tend to reflect a value system that challenges Western precepts head-on, not only in the structure of the kinship system but in the ceremonies and rituals considered important in the marriage process. Such a system provides fertile ground for human rights-based critiques. This essay questions whether these are always legitimate. Where there is no clear constitutional ground for ousting a particular practice or institution (as when, objectively, it causes no demonstrable harm) the courts are urged to have regard to considerations that will protect the practice even where it is considered 'unusual' by the dominant culture.[15] One of the considerations may well be the notion of human dignity.

Notes

Introduction

1 The conference on 'Cultural Transformations in Africa: Legal, Religious and Human Rights Issues' was held at the Centre for African Studies, University of Cape Town from 11 to 13 March 1997. It was organised by the Centre for African Studies of the University of Cape Town and the Emory Law School, Emory University, and was funded by the Ford Foundation.

2 'The Commission further recommended that the traditional subjection of customary law to the standards of justice, good sense and morality of "white" colonial judges (the "repugnancy clause" in the reception statutes) should be turned on its head by means of a provision that the received common law and principles of equity should not be "repugnant to Basic Principles of national Land Policy and principles of justice, fairness and equity held in common by Tanzanian communities."'

Chapter One

1. The use of the term 'the West' is almost automatic to indicate an unexamined conglomerate of the United States and Europe and like offshoots. This usage, which lumps together so many very different histories, cultures and state practices, is analysed below. I use it here partly to draw attention to the fact that no one would now dare to use the term 'the East' is such a manner Occidentalising is discussed further below.

2. This is particularly the case where larger cultural formations are invoked. Different considerations may, in addition, be present where culture is invoked by the Westernised leaders of small indigenous peoples, because in these cases the claims about culture are a necessary part of the claims to resources (see Chanock 1998).

3. We should note, however, that one of the most important struggles over the representations of culture in recent times was fought between France and the United States

in the recent World Trade Organisation negotiations.

4. I use the verb form rather than the nouns – orientalism and occidentalism – in order to emphasise that I am describing a constant, active (and necessary) process in trans-cultural studies, and not something that can be noted, analysed or put aside.

5. Kidd wrote: 'Dawn is breaking on the Dark Continent, and the Kafirs are stirring in their sleep. Democratic Individualism is disturbing the Socialism that has reigned undisputed for ages.' For the political right a century ago communalism was in the past; for the left it was in the future. Now, it has simply been shunted sideways to neither past nor future, but to a timeless realm of culture. Kidd's interest was in con-tributing to the politically central debate in the West over the struggle between col-lectivity and individuality. While much that is written now appears to take for grant-ed the triumph of a form of individualism which is associated with the West, we might note that A. V. Dicey's classic *Lectures on the Relation between Law and Public Opinion in England during the 19th Century*, which was first published in 1905, was about the struggle between individualism and collectivism in England and assumed, gloomily, that collectivism had won.

6. Most notoriously, they have been able to demonstrate their group character by their ability to organise for war. To take the case of Britain, an allegedly highly 'individu-alistic' Anglo-Saxon society, national sentiment and group cohesion were such that millions joined the armed forces *voluntarily* in World War One and went to their deaths. On a more positive note, one might point to the long and (sometimes) suc-cessful history of solidarity in the trade union movement. Of course, the issue is not really about the differences between individualism and communalism, but about the differences between the *types of groups* that are important at different times in history and in different state and social structures. Currently in many societies 'communal' groups provide what the state does not in vital areas like physical security and social welfare.

7. Cf. Frederic Jameson: 'a profound modification of the public sphere needs to be theorised, the emergence of a new realm of image reality which is both fictional (nar-rative) and factual ... and which now – like the former classical 'sphere of culture' – becomes semi-autonomous and floats above reality, with this fundamental historical difference that in the classical period reality persists independently of that senti-mental and romantic 'cultural sphere' whereas today it seems to have lost that sep-arate mode of existence, culture impacting back on it in ways that make any in-dependent and as it were non- or extra-cultural form or reality problematical ...' (see Matterlart 1991: 210–11).

8. Much international advertising is simply of brand names rather than products. Consumers of televised sport will be well aware of this. International soccer, espe-cially in international club competitions, is often played in virtually empty grounds but televised against the same background of international brand names regardless of what country the game is in. Entire competitions have (blessedly) been called into being simply at the behest of sponsors. This is a long way from imagining, say, the 'Iranian revolution sponsored by ...' but the links between public events and brand names have been established. Public discourses and space are increasingly given

over to 'images' (Mattelart 1991: 210).

9.   The Asian version of the rights debate has been frequently described. Asian govern-
     ments such as those of China, Singapore, Indonesia and Malaysia have been the most
     scornfully explicit in their rejection of Western versions of rights. In doing so they
     have laid particular stress on culture, and claimed a culture for Asia based on author-
     ity, religion, duty, community and family, depicting the West as individualist and in
     a state of moral and social decay because of the decline of the authority vested in
     state and family. (This latter critique is, of course, also widely deployed in the Islamic
     world.) The eerie echoings between the ruling elites of anti-democratic states in Asia,
     Africa and the Middle East have more to do with shared political insecurities than
     with cultures.

10. Chazan observes that 'Both statism (which invites populism) and state decay (which
     evokes localism) stymie the growth of civil society' (1994: 278). The weakness of the
     state, she suggests, is a factor in slowing the growth of organisations committed to
     its reform, as the state is not seen as the source of advantage. Current circumstances
     have led, instead, to the growth of religious organisations 'antithetical' to the concept
     of civil society.

Chapter Two

1.   In this regard, I think, Mamdani (1996: 111ff) probably exaggerates the civilising
     mission of what he calls civil law in Africa.

2.   Discussing the concept of 'public lands' in the Land Ordinance, Van Rees, the
     Belgian representative to the Permanent Mandates Commission observed: 'It appears
     to be more likely that he [the draftsman] did not wish to establish a legal relation
     between what are known as "public lands" and the State, and that consequently he
     had in view merely an *administrative relation* in the sense that these lands have been
     placed in their entirety under Government control' (quoted in Lyall 1973: 86).

3.   There was a plethora of agriculture by-laws providing criminal sanctions against
     breaches. They dealt mainly with mandatory provisions to cultivate specified acres
     of food and cash crops, quality controls, 'good' husbandry, etc. This practice con-
     tinued into the post-colonial era (see Shivji 1987).

4.   This is precisely the kind of dilemma which gives rise to the debate between radical
     reformers who advocate working through law, and revolutionaries who posit an ulti-
     mate overthrow of the state. In the 1970s and 1980s these debates were much more
     prominent than they are today. In the human rights context the whole development
     of social action litigation in India, now spreading in other Asian jurisdictions,
     revolves around this tension (see Cottrell 1993).

5.   The phrase 'unqualified good' comes from E. P. Thompson and arose during the
     debate in Britain in the early 1980s in reaction to Margaret Thatcher's onslaught on
     civil liberties.

6.   The confusion between the vesting of radical title in the state and the inherent pow-
     ers of eminent domain is even more pronounced in Mukoyogo and Rutinwa (1994).

7.   In the post-Arusha draft Bill, this is now cl. 58, which has been modified to allow

vesting of jurisdiction of the village council over land in the district council or the Commissioner as an ultimate decision at the discretion of the Minister. The point of principle made in the text, however, remains.

8. This study shows that the so-called decentralisation process stifled and muffled local participation, whether direct or indirect, through elected representatives. It was the decentralised officials of the central government and party functionaries who reigned supreme in decision-making bodies.

9. In this respect, Mazrui's succinct comparison between the practitioners of Western and customary law is very apposite. The practitioners of customary law, he says, 'do not constitute a formal liberal profession (attorneys, solicitors and barristers). Traditional experts of customary law are elders or experienced members of the community, normally without formal qualifications. Nor is there formal licensing for indigenous legal practice. Customary law is much less of a livelihood or money-making occupation than the kind of legal practice which came with Western colonisation.

    'At the other extreme is precisely the legacy which came with Western culture. Under this legacy, one becomes a lawyer by formal training at a university or (where imperially appropriate) an Inn of Court. Laws are codified and precisely formulated in writing. The precise language of the law is often as important as the spirit of the law. Every word matters in the text of the law, or the texts of previous judgments. On the whole, Western law is rooted in the written tradition rather than the oral – although oratorical skills in court are often of considerable relevance. Under the Western umbrella, practitioners of the law are a professional money-making fraternity with some control over qualifications necessary for practice. They also help decide the ethics which are to govern the profession – including a role in awarding or withdrawing licences to practise.' (1989: 252–3)

10. See D. North 1990: 99. The paragraph quoted reads: 'Once a development path is set on a particular course, the network externalised, the learning process of organisations, and the historically derived subjective modelling of the issues reinforces the course ... We cannot understand today's choices ... without tracing the incremental evolution of institutions.'

11. The immediate potential investment that is expected in this sector is from Afrikaner agri-business in South Africa, which seems to be moving northwards. What investment from this source could mean to the economy, politics and society of Tanzania might be gauged from Chossudovsky's article (1996) which analyses the Afrikaner entry into Mozambique.

Chapter Three

1. Critics within the critical legal studies movement ('Crits') characterised their deconstructive critique of rights as 'trashing.' The term usefully captured not only a belief that 'negative, critical activity [was] the only path that might lead to a liberated future' but also the notion that certain ideological constructs must be 'demystified' (Freeman 1978).

2. Some critical race theorists have argued that civil rights discourse was limited from

the start in its elevation of integrationism's limited conception and the rejection of a broader view of race and racism contained within the nationalists' perspective on race.

3. It must be noted that the intervention staged here was only formally positioned as individual versus group. It functioned more directly as a protection of the group expectations of whites. Cheryl Harris has analysed the court's role in protecting and insulating white rights through law – including civil rights law – in 'Whiteness as Property,' reprinted in Crenshaw et al. 1995.

4. Similarly, An-Na'im argues against abandonment and for creative engagement in the context of Islamic law, claiming that the best way to maintain the achievement of women and to resist regression is to forward an alternative Islamisation through reformation of Shari'a. 'Islam is too powerful a political and cultural force to abandon to fundamentalists' (An-Na'im 1987). See also Engle's description of the approach of feminist critics who provide 'self-conscious approaches and nuanced understandings of human rights law and discourse' (Engle 1992).

Chapter Four

1. In earlier versions, this essay has benefited considerably from discussions with Tanika Sarkar, Radhika Singha, Geetanjali Gangoli and Javeed Alam. The quarrelsome debates in the Working Group on Women's Rights have been invaluable in redefining my horizons. My visit to South Africa, for which I am grateful to Abdullahi An-Na'im and Mahmood Mamdani, brought me in touch with vital and lively debates on similar issues – most memorable have been conversations with Ebrahim Moosa, Faried Esack, Soraya Bosch and Talal Asad. My stint at the Centre for the Study of Developing Societies gave me the intellectual challenge of closely interacting with some exciting minds, Ashis Nandy, Shiv Vishwanathan and Ravi Sundaram in particular. Finally, I am grateful for the continuing conversation with Aditya Nigam.

2. In a comment made at the conference at which this essay was originally presented.

3. Hindu right-wing parties and cultural organisations have, particularly since the 1980s, made a consistent demand for a UCC, on the ground that Hindus have willingly reformed their personal law through the Hindu Code Bills passed in 1955–6, while Muslims continue to retain their personal laws unchanged. In this argument, Muslims are characterised both as backward (as opposed to the progressive Hindus) and a threat to national integrity because they resist becoming part of one set of national laws.

4. This is a case which turned the tide of the UCC debate in many ways. In 1985 the Supreme Court awarded maintenance from her husband to a divorced Muslim woman, Shah Bano, under Section 125 of the Criminal Procedure Code, which is meant to prevent vagrancy. However, the judgment contained gratuitous references to Muslim personal law as being discriminatory to women, although in this particular case, it was the secular Criminal Procedure Code, applicable to all communities, which was at issue. The judgment was protested by sections of the Muslim com-

munity, which claimed that it contravened Muslim personal law. The issue snow-balled, with the Hindu right-wing urging the immediate implementation of a UCC to override the Muslim personal law. In the face of this, the initial feminist response to the conservative reaction from the Muslim community had to be modified. At this time, in the mid-1980s, the communalisation of the polity had already become more evident, with the Hindu right-wing stepping up their campaign for the demolition of the Babri Mosque, on the site of which they claimed a temple had stood four centuries ago. The government had recently allowed Hindu worship at the temple on that site, previously closed for years on a court order. In this climate, with minority communities, particularly Muslims, feeling more insecure, it was impossible for feminists to simply hold on to their demand for a UCC, which by now had acquired strongly communal overtones. Soon after the Shah Bano judgment, under pressure from her community, Shah Bano herself revised her position, declaring that she had not understood the issue earlier. Finally in 1987, the government passed the Muslim Women (Protection of Rights upon Divorce) Act, overturning the judgment, and removing Muslim women from the purview of Section 125 of the Criminal Procedure Code. This was widely understood by women's and democratic rights groups to be an act of 'balancing communalisms' – opening the locks on the Hindu temple at the site of the Babri Mosque, followed by the Muslim Women's Bill. See Kumar 1993.

5. The Directive Principles, part IV of the Constitution, are non-justiciable and are only meant to be guidelines for the state. Other provisions like the right to work and to education are also found in this part of the Constitution – Part IV really reflects the ideal future of the Indian state as envisaged by the nationalist leadership.

Chapter Six

1. De Coulanges (1956: 186) points out that among the Greeks, Romans and Hindus, law was first a part of religion.

2. In Muslim political thought there is an adage which says: '*al-din wa'l dawla tawaman* – religion and state are twins.' Here religion refers to the juro-moral code (law) and the state as the social order.

3. Besides what is happening in the Muslim world, the reassertion of Hindu fundamentalism in India – and with it the Hinduisation of the political and legal order – comes to mind, as well as the conflict between Buddhist Sinhalese and Hindu Tamils in Sri Lanka's on-going civil war.

4. Mamdani (1976: 83) shows that religiously based caste associations were the *modus operandi* for the organisation of relations with the state in Central Africa, especially Uganda.

5. Names of church leaders such as the Anglican Archbishop Desmond Tutu, as well as influential members of the Dutch Reformed Church such as Allan Boesak and Beyers Naudé, became household names at home and also enjoyed international standing in the world anti-apartheid forums.

6. From the Preamble:

We therefore, through our freely elected representative, adopt this Constitution as the supreme law of the Republic so as to – …

Heal the divisions of the past and establish a society based on democratic values, social justice and fundamental human rights;

Lay the foundations for a democratic and open society in which government is based on the will of the people and every citizen is equally protected by law …

May God protect our people.

Nkosi Sikelel' iAfrika … God bless South Africa.

Chapter Seven

1. The Universal Declaration of Human Rights, adopted in 1948, embodied a philosophy of human rights that was directly descended from the religious, social and political struggles in England and France between the seventeenth and nineteenth centuries, and in the United States of America for part of that time. It marked the culmination of the fight against absolutism whose early beginnings can be traced back to the ideas of Hobbes and Locke, and to such significant events in European and American history as the trial of Charles I in 1649, the Virginia Declaration of Rights in 1776 and the French Declaration of 1789. These moves developed against the background of strong natural law and the contract theory ideas, and the present-day international human rights ideal still bears the imprint of those origins (see Nhlapo 1989: 1–20).

2. It has sometimes been argued that perceived Third World hostility to human rights as a 'Western construct' may be true of civil and political rights but can hardly be said to be true of social and economic rights, which after all address precisely those issues that are of concern to poor people. The point may be conceded; but it should be pointed out, nevertheless, that it is invariably the so-called first-generation rights which will be invoked in debates involving a clash of cultures.

3. Robert Thornton (1988) makes a telling point about what culture *does*: it creates boundaries. 'Boundaries are created and maintained when people observe, learn, and finally internalise the rituals and habits of speech, the dispositions and dress of their bodies and modes of thought to the extent that they become entirely automatic and unconscious. These boundaries come to seem uniquely real and permanent. Their creation through cultural means is only obvious when we step outside our normal day-to-day interactions.'

4. Reference to 'shared ideas and meanings' should not be construed as blindness to the dangers of positing the culture of any community as a given. There is ample evidence that a contemporary definition of culture must take into account the nature of culture as a phenomenon that is essentially contested and processual rather than uniform and static (see Kaganas and Murray 1994: 409–33; Cheater 1989: ii; Nhlapo 1995: 226–32).

5. See Nhlapo 1992. This seems to be borne out by Roosens (1989), quoted by Bennett (1995: 8–9), who notes that this conscious choice is invariably exercised by people

who have managed to achieve a certain distance from their own culture.

6. See generally Nhlapo 1992, where statistics tracing rising levels of urbanisation among black South Africans, the breakdown of the extended family and traditional authority, and other indicators of social transformation are questioned as not being revealing enough about African allegiance to some traditional institutions and practices which are closely linked with identity. The concern is posed thus: 'Studies which go beneath the surface would be more convincing. For instance, investigations into how the "new" blacks view the question of relatives would be more illuminating than the information that they live in town, in a house with running water, in a nuclear-family model, and have developed a taste for classical music. One would want to know whether the duty to advance less fortunate kin has been abandoned, or whether it is now discharged with a cheque (i.e. boarding school for the nieces, or a catering contract as contribution to a cousin's wedding). Is attendance at funerals rated as an obligation or a courtesy, and so on?'

7. Polygyny is that version of polygamy where a man may marry more than one woman; polyandry is the system allowing a woman to have more than one husband.

8. This is a system in which relatives are reckoned largely according to the *level* that they occupy on the family tree, regardless of sex. Thus when someone refers to a female as 'my father' they may mean nothing more dramatic than that she, after the death of the father in question, remains as 'the only surviving sibling in my father's family'.

9. For a discussion of the creation of 'artificial' kinship ties in African tradition see Nhlapo 1993.

10. The transfer (or any negotiation regarding the transfer) of cattle, other forms of livestock or other valuable consideration from the family of the groom to the family of the bride as part of the marriage process.

11. On 'othering', see Todorov (1984: Chs. 1 and 2). I am grateful to my student Sarudzayi Njerere for bringing this work to my attention in her research essay, 'Law and "Othering,"' submitted in fulfilment of the requirements of the course South African Political Thought and Traditions at the University of Cape Town, 1994.

12 Perhaps the single most quoted obstacle to political reconciliation and social bridge-building across the ethnic divide in South Africa is the perception by many black people that their fellow citizens of European cultural orientation have made up their minds that nothing 'African' can make a positive contribution to the value system of a new South Africa. Such resentment is found in defensive statements such as: 'No one who cannot be bothered to pronounce my name correctly has the right to lecture me about morality' or, even more common, 'I cannot be told how to marry and found a family by someone who does not consider his grandmother's sister to be a close relative'.

13. This is probably an unexpected use of arguments based on human dignity. It is more common to deploy the concept of human dignity in defence of individual rights, a task for which it is well suited since the express objective of the international human rights system is to protect human dignity. It appears to me, with respect, that in those societies where the tensions between the individual and the group ethic are

still working themselves out, it is a legitimate use of human dignity to argue that it is no less important to groups than it is to individuals.

14. On the impact of various forms of cultural relativism on human rights arguments, see Teson (1985: 889).

15. Theoretically this covers all traditional practices and institutions, from circumcision to *lobolo*, from courtship rules to mourning rituals. It presupposes an approach according to which each practice and institution is individually assessed on its merits, taking into account its origin, its function and its mode of expression. It also presupposes that the courts' protection should not be available for those practices and institutions which are found, objectively, to cause harm or to violate human rights in other ways (see Nhlapo 1991: 141–5). For suggestions regarding how the vexed question of polygyny might be dealt with, see Nhlapo 1994–5: 49–71.

References

Chapter One

Carrier, J. G. ed. (1995) *Occidentalism: Images of the West*. Oxford: Clarendon Press.

Chanock, M. L. (1998) 'Globalisation: Culture: Property' in Couvalis, G. et al. (eds.) *Cultural Heritage: Values and Rights*. Adelaide: Flinders University Press.

Mattelart, A. (1991) *Advertising International: The Privatisation of Public Space*. London and New York: Routledge.

Migdal, J. S. (1988) *Strong Societies and Weak States: State–Society Relations and State Capabilities in the Third World*. Princeton: Princeton University Press.

Migdal, J. S., A. Kohli and V. Shue (eds.) (1994) *State Power and Social Forces:. Domination and Transformation in the Third World*. Cambridge: Cambridge University Press.

Nader, L. (1989) 'Orientalism, Occidentalism and the Control of Women'. *Cultural Dynamics* 2, 323–55.

Orwell, G. and M. Rosenfeld (ed.) (1994) *Constitutionalism, Identity, Difference, and Legitimacy: Theoretical Perspectives*. Durham, NC: Duke University Press.

Sklar, R. L. and C. S. Whitaker (1991) *African Politics and Problems in Development*. Boulder and London: Lynne Rienner.

Spencer, J. (1995) 'Occidentalism in the East: The Uses of the West in the Politics and Anthropology of South Asia', in Carrier (1995).

Chapter Two

Chanock, M. (1991) 'A Peculiar Sharpness: An Essay on Property in the History of Customary Law in Colonial Africa.' *Journal of African History*, 32.3, 65–88.

Cottrell, J. (1993) 'Third Generation Rights and Social Action Litigation' in S. Adelman and A. Paliwala (eds.) *Law and Crisis in the Third World*. London: Hans Zell.

Coulson, A. (1982) *Tanzania: A Political Economy*. Oxford: Oxford University Press.

Chossudovsky, M. (1996) 'Apartheid Moves to Sub-Saharan Africa.' *Third World Resurgence*, 76.

Fine, B. (1984) *Democracy and the Rule of Law: Liberal Ideals and Marxist Critique*. London: Pluto Press.

Ghai, Y. 1986. 'The Rule of Law, Legitimacy and Governance.' *International Journal of Sociology of Law*, 14, 179–208.

Lyall, A. B. (1973) 'Land Law and Policy in Tanganyika.' LLM dissertation, University of Dar es Salaam.

MacAuslan, P. (1996a) 'Making Law Work: Restructuring Land Relations in Africa.' Third Alistair Berkeley Memorial Lecture given at the London School of Economics, May 1996 (unpublished).

MacAuslan, P. (1996b) 'A Draft of a Bill for the Land Act.' Dar es Salaam: Ministry of Lands, Housing and Urban Development.

MacAuslan, P. (1996c) Clause-by-Clause Commentary on the Draft Bill for the Land Act.' Dar es Salaam: Ministry of Lands, Housing and Urban Development.

Mafeje, A. (1995) 'Theory of Democracy and the African Discourse: Breaking Bread with my Fellow-Travellers' in E. Cole and J. Ibrahim (eds.) *Democratisation Processes in Africa*. Dakar: CODESRIA.

Mamdani, M. (1996) *Citizen and Subject: Contemporary Africa and the Legacy of Late Colonialism*. Princeton: Princeton University Press.

Mazrui, A. A. (1989) 'Post-colonial Society and Africa's Triple Heritage of Law: Indigenous, Islamic and Western Tendencies' in N. MacCormick and Z. Bankowski (eds.) *Enlightenment, Rights and Revolution*. Aberdeen: Aberdeen University Press.

Meek, C. K. (1946) 'A Note on Crown Lands in the Colonies.' *Journal of Comparative Legislation and International Law*, 28.

Mukoyogo, M. C. and B. Rutinwa. (1994) 'Comments on the Report of the Law Tenure Study Group and Professor Shivji's Comments Thereon.' University of Dar es Salaam (unpublished).

Mushi, S. S. (1978) 'Popular Participation and Regional Development Planning: The Politics of Decentralised Administration.' *Tanzania Notes and Records*, 83, 63–97.

North, D. (1990) *Institutions, Institutional Change and Economic Performance*. Cambridge: Cambridge University Press.

Nyerere, J. K. (1966) *Freedom and Unity: A Selection from Writings and Speeches*. Dar es Salaam: Oxford University Press.

Okoth-Ogendo, H. W. (1991) 'Constitutions without Constitutionalism' in I. G. Shivji (ed.) *State and Constitutionalism: An African Debate on Democracy*. Harare: SAPES.

Shaidi, L. P. (1985) 'Explaining Crime and Social Control in Tanzania Mainland: An Historical Socio-economic Perspective.' PhD thesis, University of Dar es Salaam.

Shivji, I. G. (1987) 'The Roots of the Agrarian Crisis in Tanzania: Theoretical

Perspectives.' *Eastern Africa Social Science Research Review*, 3.1.

Shivji, I. G. (1992) 'The Politics of Liberalisation in Tanzania: Notes on the Crisis of Ideological Hegemony' in H. Campbell and H. Stein (eds.) *Tanzania and the IMF: The Dynamics of Liberalisation*. Boulder: Westview.

Shivji, I. G. (1994) 'A Legal Quagmire: Tanzania's Regulation of Land Tenure (Establishment of Villages) Act, 1992.' *Pastoral Land Tenure Series*, 5. London: IIED.

Shivji, I. G. (1995) 'The Rule of Law and Ujamaa in the Ideological Formation of Tanzania.' *Social and Legal Studies*, 4.2; 147–174.

Shivji, I. G. (1996) 'Grounding the Debate on Land: National Land Policy and its Implications.' Paper presented at the workshop on land, January 1996.

Shivji I. G. (1997) 'Constructing a New Rights Regime: Promises, Problems and Prospects.' *Utafiti, New Series*, 3.1.

Tanzania, United Republic. (1992) *Report of the Presidential Commission of Enquiry into Land Matters*, Vols. 1 and 2. Uppsala. Published in association with the Scandinavian Institute of African Studies.

Tanzania, United Republic. (1993) *Draft of the National Land Policy* (Ministry of Land, Housing and Urban Development). Dar es Salaam.

Tanzania, United Republic. (1995) *National Land Policy* (Ministry of Land, Housing and Urban Development). Dar es Salaam.

Williams, D. V. (1982) 'State Coercion against Peasant Farmers: The Tanzanian State.' *Journal of Legal Pluralism*, 20.

Chapter Three

Crenshaw, K. (1988) 'Race, Reform and Retrenchment: Transformation and Legitimation in Antidiscrimination Law.' *Harvard Law Review*, 101. 1331.

Crenshaw, K. (1989) 'Demarginalizing the Intersection of Race and Sex: A Black Feminist Critique of Antidiscrimination Doctrine, Feminist Theory and Antiracist Politics.' *Chicago Legal Forum*, 139.

Crenshaw, K. (1993) 'Whose Story Is It Anyway? Feminist and Antiracist Appropriations of Anita Hill' in Toni Morrison (ed.) *Race-ing Justice, Engendering Power: Essays on Anita Hill, Clarence Thomas, and the Construction of Social Reality*. New York: Pantheon Books.

Crenshaw, K. (1995) *Critical Race Theory: The Key Writings that Formed the Movement*. New York: New Press.

Freeman, A. (1978) 'Legitimizing Racial Discrimination Through Antidiscrimination Law: A Critical Review of Supreme Court Doctrine.' *Minnesota Law Review*, 62.1049.

Gabel, R. (1984) 'The Phenomenology of Rights-Consciousness and the Pact of the Withdrawn Selves.' *Texas Law Review*, 62.1563.

Kennedy, D. (1997) *A Critique of Adjudication: Fin de Sièle*. Cambridge, Mass.: Harvard University Press.

Trubek, D. and M. Galanter (1974) 'Scholars in Self-Estrangement: Some Reflection on the Crisis of Law and Development Studies in the United States.' *Wisconsin Law Review*, 4.1062.

Tushnet, M. (1984) 'An Essay on Rights.' *Texas Law Review*, 62.1363.

Chapter Four

Agnes, Flavia. (1994) 'Women's Movement within a Secular Framework: Redefining the Agenda.' *Economic and Political Weekly*, May: 1123–28.

Ahmad, Imtiaz. (1995) 'Personal Laws: Promoting Reform from Within.' *Economic and Political Weekly*, 11 November.

Basu, T., P. Datta, S. Sarkar, T. Sarkar and S. Sen. (1993) *Khaki Shorts and Saffron Flags: A Critique of the Hindu Right*. Delhi: Orient Longman.

Bayly, C. A. (1994) 'Returning the British to South Asian History: The Limits of Colonial Hegemony'. *South Asia*, 27.

Chakrabarty, Dipesh. (1995) 'Modernity and Ethnicity in India: A History for the Present.' *Economic and Political Weekly*, 30 December.

Cossman, Brenda and Ratna Kapur. (1992) 'Secularism: Benchmarked by the Hindu Right.' *Economic and Political Weekly*, 21 September.

Government of India. (1974) *Towards Equality: Report of the National Committee on the Status of Women in India*. New Delhi: Ministry of Education and Social Welfare.

Government of India. (1975) *Status of Women in India: A Synopsis of the Report of the National Committee on the Status of Women, 1971–4*. New Delhi: The Indian Council of Social Science Research.

Kumar, Radha. (1993) *The History of Doing: An Illustrated Account of Movements for Women's Rights and Feminism in India*. London and New York: Verso.

Majlis et al. (1996) 'Plea to Reframe the Agenda.' Letter circulated to women's groups and individuals, May 1996.

Mamdani, Mahmood. (1996) *Citizen and Subject: Contemporary Africa and the Legacy of Late Colonialism*. Princeton, New Jersey: Princeton University Press, 1996.

Sobhaan, Salma. (1996) 'Religious Laws Are Not Merely Retrograde but Can Also be Very Retrograde for Women.' *Communalism Combat*, 5–6 April.

Taylor, Charles. (1986) 'Human Rights: The Legal Culture' in *Philosophical Foundations of Human Rights*. Paris: UNESCO and International Institute of Philosophy.

Chapter Five

Abdullah, H. J. (1993) 'Transition Politics and the Challenge of Gender in Nigeria'. *Review of African Political Economy*, 56.

Abdullah, H. J. (1994) *Between Emancipation and Subordination: A Study of the Women's Movement in Nigeria*. Washington: Ford Foundation.

Abdullah, H. J. (1995) 'The Nigerian Women's Movement and "Wifeism" as a State Response' in Amrita Basu (ed.) *The Challenge of Local Feminisms: Women's Movements in a Global Perspective*. Boulder: Westview Press.

Abdullah, H. J. (1996) 'Nigerian Muslim Women: Organising for Change.' Paper presented at a workshop on Women and Sufism organised by the Scandinavian Institute of African Studies, Uppsala, Sweden, September.

Azzam, M. (1996) 'The Islamists and the State under Mubarak' in Abdel Salam Sidahmed and A. Ehteshami (eds.) *Islamic Fundamentalism*. Boulder: Westview Press.

Babangida, M. (1991) Text of a speech at the 1991 Africa prize for Leadership for the Sustainable End of Hunger. Reproduced in the *New Nigerian*, 13 October.

Birai, U. M. (1993) 'Islamic Tajdid and the Political Process in Nigeria' in Martin E. Marty and R.S. Appleby (eds.) *Fundamentalisms and the State: Remaking Polities, Economies, and Militance*. Chicago: University of Chicago Press.

Dennis, Carolyne. (1987) 'Women and the State in Nigeria: The Case of the Federal Military Government 1984–85' in Haleh Afshar (ed.) *Women, State and Ideology*. London: Macmillan.

Ibrahim, J. (1991) 'Religion and Political Turbulence in Nigeria.' *Journal of Modern African Studies*, 29.1: 115–36.

Ibrahim, J. (1989) 'The Politics of Religion in Nigeria: The Parameters of the 1987 Crisis in Kaduna State.' *Review of African Political Economy*, 45–46: 65–82.

Imam, A. M. (1993a) 'Politics, Islam, and Women in Kano, Northern Nigeria' in Valentine Moghadam (ed.) *Identity Politics and Women: Cultural Reassertions and Feminisms in International Perspective*. Boulder: Westview Press.

Imam, A. M. (1993b) 'The Dynamics of Winning: An Analysis of Women in Nigeria (WIN)' in Chandra Mohanty and J. Alexander (eds.) *Third World Feminism*. London: Basil Blackwell.

Joseph, S. (1993) 'Family and Women's Human Rights.' *South Asian Bulletin*, 13.1/2: 148–151.

Kabir, Z. (1985) *Women's Liberation: Myth or Reality*. Mimeo, Kano.

Kerr, J. (ed.) (1994) *Ours by Right: Women's Human Rights*.

Kukah, M.H. (1993) *Religion, Politics and Power in Northern Nigeria*. Ibadan: Spectrum Publishers.

Marshall, R. (1993) 'Power in the Name of Jesus.' *Review of African Political Economy*, 52: 21–37.

Mba, N. (1982). *Nigerian Women Mobilized: Women's Political Activity in Southern Nigeria 1900–1965*. Berkeley: University of California Press.

Moghadam, V. (1990) *Gender, Development and Policy: Toward Equity and Empowerment*. UNU, WIDER.

Olukoshi, A. O. (ed.) (1993) *The Politics of Structural Adjustment in Nigeria*. London: James Currey.

Olukoshi, A. O. (1994) 'The State and the Civilian Liberties Movement in Nigeria, 1985–1993.' Paper presented at the Conference on Dimensions of Economic and Political Reform in Contemporary Africa, organised by the Scandinavian Institute of African Studies, held in Kampala, Uganda, 8–12 April.

Shettima, A. K. (1991) 'Engendering Nigeria's Third Republic.' Paper presented at the CODESRIA Conference on the Politics of Structural Adjustment in Africa. Dakar, September.

Tomasevski, K. (1993) *Women and Human Rights*. London: Zed Books.

Women in Nigeria Editorial Committee. (1985) *The WIN Document: The Conditions of Women in Nigeria and Policy Recommendations to 2000 AD*. Zaria: Ahmadu Bello University.

Yusuf, B. (1991) 'Hausa–Fulani Women: The State of the Struggle' in Catherine Coles and B. Mack (eds.) *Hausa Women in the Twentieth Century*. Madison: University of Wisconsin Press.

Chapter Six

Asad, Talal. (1993) *Genealogies of Religion: Discipline and Reasons of Power in Christianity and Islam*. Baltimore and London: The Johns Hopkins University Press.

Berman, Harold J. (1993) *Faith and Order: The Reconciliation of Law and Religion*. Atlanta, Georgia: Scholars Press.

Carpenter, Gretchen. (1995) 'Beyond Belief: Religious Freedom under the South African and American Constitutions.' *Tydskrif vir Hedendaagse Romeins-Hollandse Reg*, 58.4.

Carter, Stephen L. (1993) *The Culture of Disbelief: How American Law and Politics Trivialise Religious Devotion*. New York: Anchor Books.

Casanova, José. (1994) *Public Religions in the Modern World*. Chicago: University of Chicago Press.

Chidester, David. (1994) 'Authentic Forgery and Forging Authenticity: Comparative Religion in South Africa.' Inaugural lecture, New Series, No. 186. Cape Town: UCT.

De Coulanges, Numa Denis Fustel. (1956) *The Ancient City*. New York: Doubleday Anchor.

De Man, Paul. (1979) *Allegories of Reading*. New Haven and London: Yale University Press.

Douzinas, Costas, Ronnie Warrington and Shaun McVeigh. (1991) *Postmodern Jurisprudence: The Law of Texts in the Texts of the Law*. London: Routledge.

Goodrich, Peter and Ronnie Warrington. (1990) 'The Lost Temporality of Law: An Interview with Pierre Legendre.' Trans. Allain Pottage. *Law and Critique*, 1.1.

Mamdani, Mahmood. (1976) *Politics and Class Formation in Uganda*. New York and London: Monthly Review Press.

Mureinik, Etienne. (1994) 'A Bridge to Where? Introducing the Interim Bill of Rights.' *South African Journal on Human Rights*, 10.

Republic of South Africa. (1996) *Constitution*.

Sullivan, Winnifred Fallers. (1994) *Paying the Words Extra: Religious Discourse in the Supreme Court of the United States*. Cambridge, Mass.: Harvard University Press.

Thompson, John B. (1990) *Ideology and Modern Culture*. Oxford: Polity Press.

World Conference on Religion and Peace – South African Chapter (WCRP-SA). (n.d.) *Declaration on Religious Rights and Responsibilities*.

Chapter Seven

Bennett, T. W. (1993) 'Human Rights and the African Cultural Tradition' in W. Schmale (ed.) *Human Rights and Cultural Diversity*. Goldbach, Germany: Keip Publishing.

Bennett, T. W. (1995) *Human Rights and African Customary Law*. Cape Town: Juta.

Cheater, A. P. (1989) 'Managing Culture en Route to Socialism: The Problem of Culture "Answering Back."' *Zambezia*, 16.

Donnelly, J. and R. Howard, (1986) 'Human Dignity, Human Rights and Political Regimes.' *American Political Science Review*, 80.3: 801–17.

Donnelly, J. (1982) 'Human Rights and Human Dignity: An Analytical Critique of Non-Western Conceptions of Human Rights.' *American Political Science Review*, 76.

Kaganas, F. and C. Murray. (1994) 'The Contest Between Culture and Equality under South Africa's Interim Constitution.' *Journal of Law and Society*, 121.4: 409–33.

Keesing, R. M. (1976) *Cultural Anthropology: A Contemporary Perspective*. New York: Holt, Rinehart and Winston.

Ngubane, H. (1991) 'On Being a Native Anthropologist: Anomalies and Opportunities.' Unpublished inaugural lecture. Cape Town: University of Cape Town.

Nhlapo, R. T. (1989) 'International Protection of Human Rights and the Conventions and the Family: African Variations on a Common Theme.' *International Journal of Law and the Family*.

Nhlapo, R. T. (1991) 'The African Family and Women's Rights: Friends or Foes?' *Acta Juridica*, 135–46.

Nhlapo, R. T. (1992) 'Culture and Women Abuse: Some South African Starting Points.' *Agenda*, 13: 5–14.

Nhlapo, R. T. (1993) 'Biological and Social Parenthood in African Perspective: The Movement of Children in Swazi Family Law' in Eekelaar and Sarcevic (eds.)

Parenthood in Modern Society: Legal and Social Issues for the Twenty-first Century. London: Martinus Nijhoff.

Nhlapo, R. T. (1994–5) 'Indigenous Law and Gender in South Africa: Taking Human Rights and Cultural Diversity Seriously.' *Third World Legal Studies*, 49–71.

Nhlapo, R. T. (1995) 'Cultural Diversity, Human Rights and the Family in Contemporary Africa: Lessons from the South African Constitutional Debate.' *International Journal of Law and the Family*, 9: 226–32.

Roosens, E. E. (1989) *Creating Ethnicity: The Process of Ethnogenesis*. California: Sage Publications.

Teson, F. (1985) 'International Human Rights and Cultural Relativism.' *Virginia Journal of International Law*, 25.

Thornton, R. (1988) 'Culture: A Contemporary Definition' in E. Boonzaier and J. Sharp (eds.) *South African Keywords*. Cape Town: David Philip.

Todorov, T. (1984) *The Conquest of America: The Question of the Other*. New York: Harper and Row.

Index

cultural authenticity 2–3, 19, 21, 27–8, 61; *see also* family and land law

cultural difference 2–4, 18–19, 21–4, 26–8, 142–4, 147–8

cultural relativism 67, 146, 148

cultural transformation 2, 6, 19–20, 22, 61, 70; *see also* transformation

Cultural Tranformation Project 71–3

culture 3–4, 8, 16–18, 24–5, 33, 35–6, 75, 139–41; African 18–21, 23, 33, 140, 142–3; as relating to family and land 34–5; as relating to gender 20, 111–12; Asian 19; defence of 3, 67, 142; in South Africa 139–43, 145, 147; use in advertising 25–7; use in describing group and political differences 2, 18, 68

culture talk 1–2, 4, 18, 68

Declaration on Religious Rights and Responsibilities 12, 123–6, 134

democracy 4–5, 10, 37, 39, 46, 75, 95, 100, 122

democratisation 75, 92, 95; *see also* reform process

difference 4, 10, 93–4; *see also* cultural difference; diversity

diversity 4–5, 9, 95; *see also* difference

elites 2–3, 21–2, 26, 28–30, 70, 72, 83, 99, 144–5

equality 4, 39, 43, 93–4, 118 147; in India 87–8, 91–2, 94; in Nigeria 11, 98, 108, 111–13; in Tanzania 34; in the USA 61, 64, 66–9, 71; *see also* gender equality

fairness 37–9, 51, 53, 55–6, 58–60

family and land law 2, 10, 34–5, 59–60, 118, 141–2; in India 94; in Tanzania 40–4, 51–3, 58

Family Support Programme (FSP) (Nigeria) 109, 117

Federation of Muslim Women's Associations in Nigeria (FOMWAN) 11, 98, 103, 107–8, 111–15

feminism 10–11, 96–8, 109, 114–15, 119

gender equality 2, 19–20, 73, 79, 82, 84–5, 87, 117–18; *see also* equality

gender justice (India) 9, 82–90

gender rights 8–9, 80, 84; within the family 10, 80, 82, 87, 91, 115, 117; women 80, 85–9, 94–5, 120; women in Nigeria 96–8, 107–15, 117, 119–20; *see also* Shah Bano case

globalisation 3, 15, 17–18, 21–2, 25, 35, 135; in advertising 24–5, 27; of constitutionalism 34

group rights 3–4, 8, 30, 75–7, 80, 84, 86, 91

'hatukushirikishwa' 5, 45–6, 60

human rights 31, 33–4, 41, 44, 61–3, 70–1, 73–4, 115, 117–20, 136–8, 142–4, 148; in Nigeria 96–8, 110–11, 114; women's 115, 117–19

Human Rights Law Network (India) 89–90

India. Acts: Christian Marriage Act of 1872 85; Hindu Marriage Act (1955) 80; Hindu Minority and Guardianship Act 80; Hindu Succession Act 80; Land Ceilings Act 94; Special Marriage Act 84

individual rights 3–4, 8, 44, 66, 77, 91–3, 95, 144

individualisation, titling and registration

(ITR) (Tanzania) 42, 46, 56–7
individualism 21–3, 29, 38; *see also* individual rights
Internal Federation of Women Lawyers (FIDA) 11, 110–11
International Financial Institutions (IFIs) 46
International Monetary Fund (IMF) 97, 99
Islamic law 38; *see also* African customary law; state law
Islamic movement 101–2; in Nigeria 102–5

Jama'atu Nasril Islam (JNI) 102
justice 4–5, 38–9, 44–5, 51, 59–60, 94–5, 132, 136–8; in Tanzania 37, 40–5, 48, 50–3, 55–7; *see also* gender justice (India)

Kenya. Acts: Land (Group Representatives) Act of 1968 57
King Jr., Martin Luther 67, 74

land rights (Tanzania) 40–1, 44, 48, 56–7
land tenure reform (Tanzania) 37, 40–3, 46–7, 57–8; dispute-settlement machinery 37, 50–3; Land Ordinance (1923) 40–2, 54–5; village adjudication 37, 51, 56–7; *see also* Tanzania. Acts
Legal Research and Resource Development Centre (LRRDC) (Nigeria) 110–11

MacAuslan, Patrick 37, 40, 45, 48, 54, 58–9
Mafeje, Archie 46

Mazrui, Ali 38
modernity 75–7, 79, 92, 127–8, 133
multiculturalism 138–9, 144

National Commission for Women (NCW) (Nigeria) 109
National Committee on the Status of Women (India) 79
National Conference of Women's Studies (Fifth: 1995, India) 78
National Council of Women's Societies (NCWS) (Nigeria) 107–8, 112–16.
national integrity (India) 79–80, 82–4, 88
National Land Policy (NLP) (Tanzania) 37, 40, 47–8, 54–5, 60
National Lands Commission (NLC) (Tanzania) 4–6, 40, 44–7, 49–53, 55, 57; recommendations 47, 49, 51, 54, 56, 58, 60
National Party of Nigeria (NPN) 116
natural law 39, 117
non-governmental organisations (NGOs) 62, 96, 110–11, 118
Nyerere, Julius 42–4

occidentalising 2–3, 16, 20–2, 24, 26, 35, 62, 137, 148
'Operation Vijji' (Tanzania) 54–5
orientalising 3, 20–2, 24, 26, 35
Overseas Development Agency (ODA) 37

Pentecostal Fellowship of Nigeria (PFN) 102
personal law 10, 12, 77–9, 82–3, 85–7, 89–91; Hindu 9, 80, 83–4; inequality of 84, 95; Muslim 83–5; reform of 85–92